CAMBRIDGE GEOGRAPHICAL TEXT BOOKS

General Editor: G. F. BOSWORTH, F.R.G.S.

JUNIOR

T0382045

CAMBRIDGE GEOGRAPHICAL TEXT BOOKS

JUNIOR

BY

A. R. CHART-LEIGH, M.Sc.

CAMBRIDGE
AT THE UNIVERSITY PRESS
1921

CAMBRIDGE
UNIVERSITY PRESS

University Printing House, Cambridge CB2 8BS, United Kingdom

Published in the United States of America by Cambridge University Press, New York

Cambridge University Press is part of the University of Cambridge.

It furthers the University's mission by disseminating knowledge in the pursuit of
education, learning and research at the highest international levels of excellence.

www.cambridge.org
Information on this title: www.cambridge.org/9781107627338

© Cambridge University Press 1921

First published 1921
First paperback edition 2014

A catalogue record for this publication is available from the British Library

ISBN 978-1-107-62733-8 Paperback

EDITOR'S NOTE

THIS Junior Book, one of a series of three Geographical text-books on the concentric system, is intended for the younger pupils in secondary schools and the older pupils in elementary schools, who are able to approach this subject for the first time through a good text-book after definite instruction in the class.

The Editor suggests that the first three chapters may form the basis of an introductory course of practical work, especially for pupils in the lower forms of secondary schools. Thus the study of contour maps in Chapter I, the plotting of isotherms and isobars in Chapter II, and the study and compilation of maps showing the distribution of plants, animals, and population will enable the teacher to revise in a practical form the work of earlier stages in this subject. The regional studies which follow give a general survey of the World, special attention being given to the British Empire, and to the effects of the late war. It is hoped that the illustrations of physical features, of the fauna and flora, and of the industries of various countries will prove of value to the young student. The exercises and questions at the end of the book have been carefully compiled and are intended to test the pupil's knowledge of his work and to develop his powers of expression. It is intended that this book should be used with a good atlas, for a knowledge of places and positions is better learnt from special maps than from a text-book.

Special thanks are due to Mr A. R. Hinks, F.R.S., who wrote the first chapter on the shape, size, and movements of the Earth.

G. F. B.

February 1921

CONTENTS

LIST OF ILLUSTRATIONS

DIAGRAMS

CHAPTER I

SHAPE, SIZE, AND MOVEMENTS OF THE EARTH

It is easy to show that the surface of the sea is round and not flat. The hull of a ship may be hidden from sight by the sea, while the masts and spars are plainly visible above it. Such an effect can be produced only by the curvature of the sea surface.

The precise size and shape of the Earth can be determined by the surveyor.

The Earth is one of the planets, and, like all the planets, it both moves round the Sun, and also spins upon itself. The first of these movements is called revolution; it takes a year for the Earth to move round the Sun. The second movement is called rotation. The Earth spins upon its axis in a day. The motion round the Sun in a year gives us the seasons; the turning in a day gives the succession of day and night.

Latitude and Longitude.

To understand what is meant by Latitude and Longitude, and the Poles and the Equator, it is well to go at once to the globe. The globe is mounted so that it spins on an axle, and the points where this axle passes through the globe's surface are the Poles. The actual Earth has not a mechanical axle to turn on; but it turns as if it had. The line on which it turns is called the Earth's axis.

On the globe we shall find a number of lines drawn direct from Pole to Pole. These are called *meridians*.

And we shall find a number of circles drawn round the globe at intervals, all parallel to one another, and all

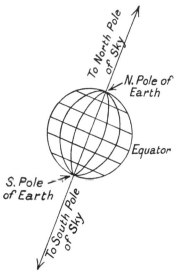

Fig. 1. The Globe—Meridians and Parallels

cutting the meridians at right angles. These circles are called the *parallels of latitude*, and the largest of them, which encircles the Earth exactly midway between the two poles, is called the *Equator*.

It must of course be understood that these lines and circles do not exist upon the real Earth; one cannot see the Equator when one crosses it. But they are useful on the globe in helping to define the positions of places by their latitude and longitude, as we shall see immediately.

It is customary to divide a circle into 360 degrees. Then if there are on the globe twenty-four meridians equally spaced, we may say that they are 15 degrees, or 15° apart. And if there were thirty-six meridians drawn they would be 10° apart. Similarly, if the parallels divide the quarter circle of 90° between the Equator and the Pole into nine equal parts, the parallels are 10° apart.

But we must not think of the meridians and parallels as confined to those lines which are ordinarily marked upon the globe. Through any point on the globe we may draw a parallel of latitude and a meridian. The distance in angle between the parallel and the Equator is called the *latitude* of the place. The angle between the meridian of the place and the meridian of Greenwich Observatory is called the *longitude* of the place, East or West of Greenwich as the case may be. Thus when we are given these quantities, the latitude and longitude of a place, we know exactly where it is upon the Earth. And it would be difficult to describe its position exactly in any other way.

Time.

Time may be measured by clocks, but how is one to know that the clocks are going at the right speed? The regular turning of the Earth upon its axis gives us a perfectly regular clock, and the astronomer makes use of this motion to tell the time by the stars and the sun.

It is clear from the globe that the time must be different in different parts of the Earth, for while it is day on one side it is night on the other.

The time is the same for all places on the same meridian, and it changes regularly with the change of longitude from Greenwich. Thus differences of longitude may very well be expressed in time, and they very often are. Thus we may say that a place is four hours west of Greenwich. And it is clear that since the whole circuit of the Equator may thus be reckoned either as 360° or as 24 hours, we change longitude in degrees into longitude in time at the rate of 15° to one hour.

And further, it is clear that the time at a place will be different from the time at another place whose longitude is not the same. And if clocks kept this local time everywhere, each town would have its own time, which would be very inconvenient in railway travelling and in all business affairs. Therefore it

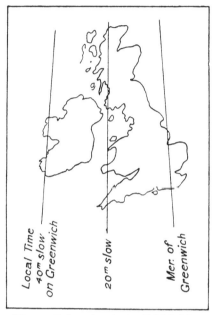

Fig. 2. Solar Time in the British Isles

is arranged by law that Great Britain keeps the time of the meridian of Greenwich. And gradually other countries have fallen in with this scheme, so that France and Belgium also keep Greenwich time; the countries of central Europe keep their clocks an hour fast on ours; the eastern United States keep five hours slow; and so on. This system is called *Standard Time*.

The Seasons.

We cannot fail to notice that the Sun at midday is very much higher in summer than in winter. His rays then fall more directly on the ground, and a square yard of ground receives a much larger share of the summer rays than of the very sloping rays of winter. Thus it is much warmer in summer than in winter, in our country.

Further, in our country, the Sun remains above the horizon much longer in summer than in winter. We have a long day and a short night; and of course the greater duration of sunshine has also the effect of making the summer hotter than the winter.

The height of the Sun at noon, and the length of the day, vary very much in different parts of the Earth, and at different times of year, so that it is rather difficult to explain in a few words exactly what happens. But we may say briefly that:

On the Equator the day and the night are always equal; the Sun goes directly overhead at noon at the times we call spring and autumn; and at other times he passes at some distance, but never a great distance from the point directly overhead, called the *Zenith*. Thus on the Equator there are no marked seasons, as with us. There may be a wet season and a dry season, but there is no warm season and cold season.

On the other hand, within the Arctic regions, the Sun disappears altogether for some months, and there is perpetual night, very cold. But to make up for this, in the Arctic summer the Sun remains above the horizon for some months, and there is perpetual day. The Sun is never very high, and so it is never very hot; but it is much warmer than might be expected, and mosquitoes make the summer almost unendurable in many places.

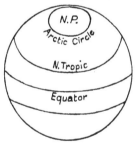

Fig. 3. Earth as seen from Sun, June 21

Twilight.

If there were no air the Sun's rays would fall in straight lines upon the Earth, and everything would be

in full sunlight or else in shadow; the sky would be
black, and the stars would be seen round about the
Sun. But, as it is, the dust in the air scatters the light,
and the Sun's rays which enter the air obliquely are
bent round, or refracted. The result of this is that we
have the pleasant diffused light of the sky, and that
when the Sun has set it does not become dark at once,
but there is twilight.

Maps.

A map is an attempt to show on a sheet of paper as
much of the shape and features of a country as can be
done within the limits of the scale of the map. Naturally,
the larger the scale, the more can be shown.

The ordinary Atlas map is on a very small scale:
perhaps one twenty-millionth of the actual size of the
Earth. Thus it is impossible to show more than the
principal features of the country—the rivers, the large
towns, the chief railways. The difficulty on all maps is
to show the mountains and hills, or what is called the
'relief' of the ground. Shading or colour to denote
height above sea-level will become confused with colour
intended to show the divisions of the land for purposes
of government—the states or the counties. Therefore
it is common to have two maps, one showing the latter,
which is called the 'political' map; and one showing
the relief of the ground, called the 'physical' map.

The physical maps in atlases are now very generally
coloured on what is called the 'layer' system, in varying
shades of green, yellow, and brown, to indicate the
height of the ground above the level of the sea.

Maps on a larger scale, such as the maps of the
Ordnance Survey, are called topographical maps, the
word topographical meaning the description of the
place. They aim at showing all the natural features
of the country—the hills, rivers, forests, lakes, and so
forth; and also the towns and villages; the roads,
canals, railways, and other means of communication
which have been made by man. Topographical maps

allow one to find the best way about the country for business or pleasure.

The chief difficulty again is to represent the relief of the ground, and many devices are used for that purpose. The slopes may be marked by *hillshading*; or lines of equal height above sea-level (*contours*) may be drawn; and in addition the ground between the contours may be tinted on the *layer system*. All these ways, separately or in combination, are found on different maps, and what is suitable for one kind of country is often very unsuitable for another.

Survey.

The method of making a regular survey of a country is somewhat complicated, and we can give only a very slight account of it here. The first thing to do is to measure a 'base' on open and level ground. That

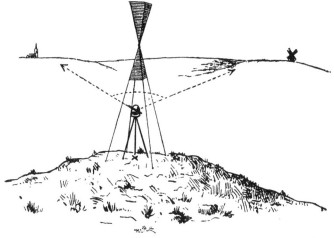

Fig. 4. Triangulation: Theodolite set up under beacon erected at one station, observing angle between two other stations on the distant church tower and windmill

gives the length of one line in feet or yards. Next, stations are chosen on the tops of hills, the towers of cathedrals, and other prominent points, well arranged over the whole country. The two ends of the base, and all these other stations, will form a network of triangles, whose angles are all measured with an instrument called the *theodolite*. Then by a long series of calculations, by trigonometry and logarithms, the surveyor finds the lengths of all the sides of the whole 'triangulation.' Next he finds by astronomical methods the latitude and longitude of one of his stations, and the true bearing of one of the sides; and then by further calculations the positions of all his other stations. This makes a framework for the map. All the detail of roads and rivers, villages and railways, may then be filled in with the instrument called the *plane table*.

All this requires great skill and good organisation. It is no use to try to survey a country in small pieces at different times, and by different people; their results will not fit together properly. Hence the maps of a country must be made by the Government, and it is one of the most important duties of a good government to make maps of a new country as soon as possible. In Great Britain the whole country is splendidly mapped by the Ordnance Survey; but in Greater Britain there is still great need of good maps, and there are immense regions of the world which are not mapped at all, except in the very roughest way and on very small scales.

Map projections.

The network of meridians and parallels which is drawn on an atlas map is called the 'projection' for the map. If one looks at the map of Asia, for example, in different atlases, one finds different ways of arranging the meridians and the parallels; and none of them gives a really true representation, because it is not possible to represent a portion of the round world accurately upon the flat sheet of the map. Either the distances, or the shapes, or the areas, or all three, are more or less wrong; and one has to use a different method for the construction of the projection, according as one is more anxious to get the distances, or the areas, or the shapes correct. On maps of small regions there is not much error, but the difficulty increases very much as one tries to represent more extensive regions of the world. Compare the world as shown on a globe with the world as shown in atlases, and you will see how different is the idea that the maps give of the relative positions of Northern Europe and North America, for example.

CHAPTER II

THE ATMOSPHERE

Overlying the Earth's surface there is a belt of gases known as the atmosphere. The lower part of the atmosphere is known as air, and is a mixture of nitrogen oxygen, water vapour, and carbon dioxide.

Effect of the Sun's heat.

The Sun's rays, which are our chief source of heat, pass through the atmosphere to the Earth's surface. This surface is heated in proportion to the inclination of the Sun's rays, and to the time during which these rays shine on the Earth's surface. As the Earth's surface becomes heated, the overlying layers of the atmosphere become heated by the radiation of heat from the rock or water surfaces.

The inclination of the Sun's rays, and therefore their heating power, is the same at all points along a parallel of latitude. The average inclination of the Sun's rays, and consequently their heating power, increases in either hemisphere as we go from the polar lands to the tropical lands (i.e. to lower latitudes). So air-temperatures increase in these directions. Within the Tropics, the heating power of the Sun's rays is always great, for the Sun shines overhead at noon on the Tropic of Cancer near the end of June, on the Equator near the end of March and September, and on the Tropic of Capricorn near the end of December, and at intervening places at intervening dates. So within the Tropics air-temperatures are always high. In all places not in the Tropics the summer season occurs when the Sun's rays have their greatest inclination, and when the Sun shines longest; the winter season is that during which the inclination of the Sun's rays is least and the duration of sunshine least.

Effect of land and water on air-temperatures.

During the summer half-year the land and water surfaces at any place are gaining heat. But the land surfaces show higher temperatures than do the water surfaces which lie on the same parallel; and therefore the air-temperatures over the land are higher than those over the sea along the same parallel. During the winter half-year the land and water surfaces at any place are losing heat. But the land-temperatures fall more than do the sea-temperatures; and therefore the air-temperatures over the land are lower than those over the sea along the same parallel. The following table shows the relative conditions of the air-temperatures over land and sea along any parallel of latitude.

Season	Air over land	Air over sea
Summer	Hot	Warm
Winter	Cold	Cool

The range in air-temperatures over the sea is much less than the range over land; and so the range over the sea is said to be equable, while that over land is said to be extreme.

Effect of altitude on air-temperatures.

The higher we go above sea-level the colder is the air. It is found that for every 300 feet ascent, there is on the average a fall of $1°$ Fahrenheit in the temperature of the air.

Movement of the air.

If two vessels, A and B, connected near their bases by a tube, are filled with water to different levels, so that the level in A is higher than the level in B, liquid will flow from *A* to *B* until a steady level is obtained. At first the pressure on the base of *A* is greater than the pressure on the base of *B*; we may say that the water flowed from the region of high pressure to the region of low pressure.

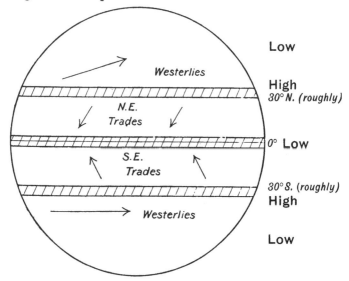

Fig. 5. Wind zones of the World

Air obeys the same laws. From a zone of high pressure, the air moves to a zone of low pressure. This moving air is called wind. Near parallel 30° in each hemisphere, there is a region of high atmospheric pressure; and over the Equator and in high northern and southern latitudes, there are three zones of low atmospheric pressure. From the two 'high' belts, air tends to move either towards the Equator or towards the Poles. But the rotation of the Earth causes all winds in the Northern Hemisphere to be deflected to the right of their expected direction of movement; and all winds in the Southern Hemisphere to be deflected to the left of their expected direction of movement. Thus, between parallel 30° N. and the Equator, the winds blow from the north-east, i.e. there are north-east winds; and between parallel 30° S. and the Equator, there are south-east winds. These north-east and south-east winds are so steady that they are known as 'trade winds.' On the northern side of parallel 30° N., there are south-west winds, while on the southern side of parallel 30° S., there are north-west winds. These winds are known as the 'westerly variables,' for in these belts winds from the west are often absent at any place for days.

In the high-pressure districts the air is descending, and in the low-pressure districts the air is ascending.

During the northern summer season (July), the winds of south-eastern Asia blow in towards a low-pressure area which lies west of India. So here, instead of the winds being north-east trade winds, there are south-west, south, and south-east winds. During the southern summer season (January), winds blow inward to north-eastern Australia—again in a direction opposite to that of the trade winds. These seasonal winds are called 'monsoons.'

Effects of winds on air-temperatures.

Air may blow over a place either from the sea or from the land. Winds from the sea bring warm air in summer and cool air in winter over places where the air should be hot in summer and cold in winter. Consequently places swept by sea breezes have equable air-temperatures. The cooling effect in summer and warming effect in winter of such winds decrease as the winds move further inland; and air-temperatures become more extreme as we go inland. The westward-moving winds within the Tropics cause places on the eastern sides of the continents to have equable air-temperatures; and the eastward-moving winds north of parallel 30° N. and south of parallel 30° S. give equable air-temperatures to the western lands.

Effects of winds on rainfall.

Water vapour is nearly always present in the air. Generally there is more water vapour in the air which overlies oceans and lakes than in the air overlying the continents. Warm air can hold more water vapour than cold air can hold. When warm air containing much water vapour is cooled, some of this vapour is turned into tiny drops of liquid. A large number of these drops, floating near the Earth's surface, form mist; when high up in the air, we say they form clouds. If these drops grow beyond a certain size, the air cannot hold them up, and the drops fall to Earth as rain. So rain is produced by the cooling of air which contains water vapour.

The cooling of air, resulting in the shedding of rain, is brought about because of :

(1) upward movement of air

(a) in the equatorial low-pressure zone,

(b) on the windward side of a mountain range;

(2) northward movement of air in the Northern Hemisphere;

(3) southward movement of air in the Southern Hemisphere.

Air when warmed can hold more water vapour, and so no rain is shed. The warming of the air, resulting in 'dry' weather, is brought about because of :

(1) downward movement of air

(a) in the high-pressure areas near parallels 30° N. and 30° S.,

(b) on the lee side of a mountain range;

(2) southward movement of air in the Northern Hemisphere ;

(3) northward movement of air in the Southern Hemisphere.

Climate.

The climate of a place is the average condition of its atmosphere. The conditions referred to are its air-temperatures and rainfall.

For some distance around each pole there is an extreme, cold, and dry climate.

The climate of the western sides of the continents which lie north of parallel 30° N., and south of parallel 30° S. varies from equable, warm, and wet to equable, cool, and wet. On the eastern side the climate is extreme and dry.

The lands within parallels 30° N. and 30° S. (except the monsoon lands and the lands near the Equator) have equable, hot, and wet climates in the east; and extreme, hot, and dry climates in the west. In the monsoon lands of south-eastern Asia and north-eastern Australia there are hot, wet summers, and warm, dry winters; and near the Equator the climate is equable, hot and very wet.

The climate near parallels 30° N. and 30° S. is very noteworthy. The western parts of the various continents near these parallels have hot, dry summers and cool, wet winters; towards the east the winters become cold. On the eastern sides of the continents near these parallels the monsoons hold sway, and thus these districts have hot, wet summers and cool, dry winters.

CHAPTER III

LIFE ON THE EARTH'S SURFACE

Plant Life.

Influence of the Earth's surface.

There is less than one-fourth of the Earth's surface available for cultivation. The highlands of the Earth are generally inaccessible, and, because of their height, they have cold climates. The lowlands of the Earth are far more important for cultivation. In valleys there is often rich soil, which produces abundant crops.

Influence of the Sun's heat.

The heat actually gained and lost by the Earth's surface affects vegetation very considerably, and this is especially noticeable in those districts where the Sun's rays shine at low angles in summer, and consequently at very low angles in winter. In such districts the rain which falls is frozen in the pores of the rock surfaces for a great part of the year ; and the ground becomes useless for the growth of any vegetation other than mosses. These very cold, barren districts are known as *tundra*. In other parts of the Earth's surface as the Sun's heating power is greater, both in summer and in winter, the soil is not subjected to such intense cold, and so there is a greater variety of vegetation.

Influence of the atmosphere.

But, altering all, we have the varying atmospheric conditions. The two features which we must specially notice are the air-temperatures and the rainfall at various parts of the Earth's surface. We find, on studying the temperature charts, that the air-temperatures rise as we travel towards the Tropics. This is not so with the rainfall, for there are great areas near each Tropic, and also at great distances from the sea, where there is little rainfall. As we travel towards the Equator from the dry districts near each Tropic, we find that the amount of rainfall increases until it becomes very great.

We know that in hot weather plants often die for want of water. So, in the areas where there is great heat and yet little rain, the natural vegetation is affected to such an extent that it dies in the dry season, leaving behind seed; and when conditions again become suitable the seed grows once more. With very little rainfall the life of the plants is short, and such districts are practically unable to support animal and human life, and hence they form the dry deserts of the World. But north and south of these dry deserts the rainfall becomes greater, and the life of the vegetation becomes longer. In these districts of low rainfall the vegetation is chiefly composed of grasses, some of which provide food for cattle and sheep. Other grasses have been cultivated in the wetter parts of the Earth for hundreds of years by human beings; and their seeds provide food of great importance to us. These 'cereals' include rye, oats, barley, wheat, maize, and rice.

Where there is enough rain all the year round to keep the soil moist, the natural vegetation grows on from year to year, producing trees. In the cold parts of the World there are tall, straight trees bearing needle-shaped leaves and seed-cones. These trees, known as *coniferous*, include the pine, fir, larch, and spruce. As the annual average air, and land-temperatures increase, the coniferous trees are gradually replaced by broad-leafed trees, which are often called *deciduous* trees. They include the oak, ash, elm, beech, and chestnut. In those parts of the hot lands which receive sufficient rainfall to support the growth of trees, there are dense forests.   The tropical forests produce valuable *hardwoods*, such as mahogany, rosewood, and teak.

Scots Pine

Zones of vegetation.

We may summarise the natural vegetation growing on the Earth's surface as follows, going from the cold regions to the tropical lands:

     barren tundra,

     coniferous forests }leading to grass regions where
     deciduous forests }the rainfall is small, i.e. at great distances from the sea,

     dry and barren deserts,
     tropical grass regions,
     tropical forests.

Animal Life.

The character and abundance of the vegetation growing on the Earth's surface directly affect animal life. The different temperatures and amounts of rainfall also cause differences in the kinds of animals inhabiting the Earth's surface. In the tundra the important animals are the reindeer, polar bear, arctic fox, and others which, by means of their thick fur, are able to withstand the intense cold. The brown bear, wolf, boar, and others wander in those parts of the more temperate regions least frequented by their hunters, the human race. Cattle, sheep, pigs, and horses are characteristic of the more peopled districts, the grass regions providing large pastures suitable for the feeding of these animals. The camel is the most important beast of burden in the dry deserts. As the rainfall increases in the tropical grass regions, the vegetation becomes thicker and larger; and it is in these regions that the greatest and wildest animals live. The best known of these are the lion, tiger, leopard, jaguar; elephant, rhinoceros, hippopotamus, giraffe, zebra; crocodile, alligator; monkey and ape. In Australia, a peculiar type of animal is found. This is the marsupial, or pouch-bearing animal, which carries its young ones in a pouch. A familiar member of this type is the kangaroo.

Birds are varied, both in size and in habits, becoming more gaily coloured as their homes become hotter. In the colder regions, many of the birds are snow-white in colour. The tropical birds are very abundant, and provide food in great quantity for the other animals living in the tropical lands.

The fish, inhabiting the fresh and salt waters of the Earth, live chiefly on sea-weeds, and on animals—insects and other fishes. The important fish from the human point of view are those fit for food; and such fish generally live in comparatively shallow water. The chief of these are cod, haddock, whiting, ling, hake; herring, pilchard, sprat, and anchovy. Of the river fish, salmon is the most important.

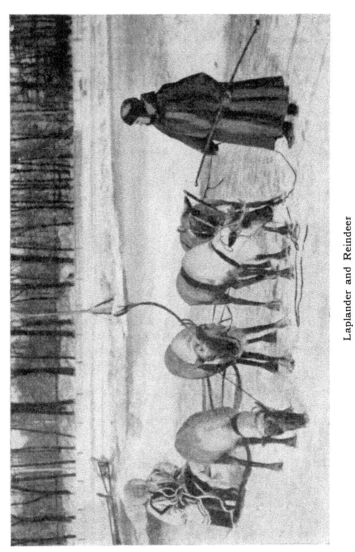

Laplander and Reindeer

Human Life.

Life in the tundra regions.

Human life is very hard in the tundra regions, because of the scanty vegetation and extreme climate. The reindeer is mankind's best friend in these regions, providing food, clothing, and means of transport. When the moss pastures are used up in one district, the owners drive their reindeer to fresh pastures, taking with them all their belongings. So these people are wanderers, or nomads, in order to keep their flocks and themselves alive. On the coastal lands of the tundra a few people live on fish.

Life in the temperate regions.

The temperate forest regions provide work for lumbermen, and in the clearings in these districts—which are now more extensive than the forests—farmers sow seeds and reap harvests wherever soils are suitable. The temperate grass regions, supporting large numbers of cattle and sheep, do not support many human lives, as few people are needed to tend large herds and flocks.

Life in the tropical regions.

The tropical grass regions are similar to the temperate ones, supporting few people in the dry parts. In the wetter parts, on the equatorial sides of the desert areas, agriculture is the chief occupation. The vegetation in the tropical forests is so dense that it makes life, both for animals and for human beings, scarcely possible. The human beings who live in these forest belts are often dwarfs, or pygmies. The chief attractions for Europeans in these lands are the valuable hardwoods and the important vegetable product, rubber.

Influence of mineral wealth on human life.

As people have explored the various parts of the Earth's surface, they have discovered rocks which contain special substances called minerals.   Among the more important minerals we may notice the native metals gold, silver, copper, mercury, and platinum; and the ores from which silver, iron, lead, tin, and zinc are obtained.   In some rocks diamonds, rubies, sapphires and other gems are found.   The minerals which probably are sought after by the greatest number of people are coal and oil.

In the mining and working of minerals a great number of people earn a livelihood.   On and near the coalfields coal can be bought at low rates.   Consequently industries requiring steam-power are carried on near to the coalfields, large numbers of people being employed in the manufacture of clothing and machinery.

CHAPTER IV

EUROPE

Position and Size.

The continent of Europe, more than 32 times the area of the British Isles, is the north-westerly part of the largest land surface of the Earth. The eastern boundary is mostly along the Ural Mts and the Ural R. The southern boundary between Europe and Asia runs along the valley of the Manich, and from the head of this river south-east to the point at which parallel 45° N. cuts the western shores of the Caspian Sea.

The Seas of Europe.

The coast of Europe on the extreme north is washed by the Arctic Ocean, and the extreme west coast by the North Atlantic Ocean. The other coastlines mark the limits of nearly land-locked inland seas. The northern seas, the Irish, North, and Baltic Seas, are remarkably shallow; while the southern seas—the Mediterranean, Black, and Caspian Seas—are all deep.

The nearly land-locked Baltic Sea freezes at its surface during the greater part of winter. The Black Sea freezes during severe winters. The Caspian Sea is very salt, and never freezes.

The Land Surface.

The North-West (or Scandinavian) Highlands lie to the north-west of the extensive lowland of Europe. The Ural Mts to the east of Europe, separate it from Asia. The plateaux of Europe include those of Spain, south-east France, and south-west Germany. The mountain ranges are the Pyrenees, Alps, Apennines, Karpathians, and Balkans.

Of the lowland areas the chief are the Central Plain and the Plains of the Po and Danube.

Divides and Rivers.

A line drawn from the mouth of the Mediterranean Sea in a north-easterly direction roughly marks the position of the high lands dividing northward-flowing rivers from those flowing southward. Of those flowing northward the chief are the Garonne, Loire, Seine, Rhine, Elbe, Oder, Vistula, Duna, Dvina, and Pechora. Of the rivers flowing southward from the main divide, the Rhone, Danube, Dniester, Dnieper, Don, and Volga are the chief.

Lakes.

On the south side of the Alps, and on the Swiss Plateau to the north of these mountains, there are many beautiful lakes. The chief of these lakes are Garda, Como, Maggiore, Geneva, Constance, Neuchatel, Lucerne. Around the Baltic Sea, there are many low-lying lakes of great extent, such as Ladoga, Onega, Vener, and Vetter; these lakes freeze over in winter.

Climate.

(*a*) Air-temperatures.

As we pass from the north of Europe with a latitude of 70° N., to the south with a latitude of a little over 35° N., we find increasing air-temperatures. The varying altitudes, especially in the south of Europe, cause the air-temperatures in these elevated districts to be lower than those of the surrounding plains and valleys.

(*b*) Rainfall.

In summer the south of Europe receives very little rain while the other parts receive much rain. The amount of the rainfall decreases as we go away from the water surfaces.

In winter all districts receive rain, the greater amounts falling in the west.

Vegetation.

(a) **Tundra.**

The tundra region occupies the northern parts of Finland and Russia. The mosses and lichens of this region are gradually replaced by small trees as the temperatures of land and air become higher southward.

(b) **The trees of Europe.**

The trees of Europe are coniferous in the north, forming the chief vegetation as far south as parallel 60° N. The pines, firs, and larches, are also found in the cold highlands of the south of Europe. South of lat. 60° N. the broader-leafed deciduous trees become more numerous, and soon the forests contain as many deciduous as coniferous trees. In the southern lands, from the south of France across to the Black Sea, the deciduous trees are most abundant. The laurel, holly, myrtle, mulberry, olive, evergreen oak, and a bushy type of pine are characteristic trees of the Mediterranean lands. The fruit trees of this southern region of summer drought and winter rain are orange, lemon, and fig. In the northern lands the apple, pear, plum, and cherry are important.

(c) **The cereals, grasses, and other cultivated plants.**

Cereals generally thrive in rather dry regions. Rye, oats, and barley will thrive in regions which are too cold and damp for other grain. Hence they are chiefly cultivated in the northern lands. Wheat, requiring a drier and warmer summer to ripen its grain, grows to perfection in France, Hungary, Italy, central and south Russia. Maize, requiring a still higher temperature, is cultivated largely in south France and south Hungary.

The temperate grass regions lie in south-east Europe, chiefly in Russia. These pasture lands support large flocks of sheep. On their western margin wheat is being cultivated.

Where the soil is too damp in the northerly European lowlands for cereal-culture, grasses are grown. These form rich meadow lands, on which large herds of cattle are fed, as in Ireland, Denmark, and Holland.

Of the other cultivated plants, flax and hemp are important in the northern parts of the Central Plain; flax being cultivated in Ireland, northern France, Belgium, Holland, and the south-east of the Baltic region. The potato is a very important and cheap foodstuff, being largely grown on the poor soils of Ireland and north-east Germany. Sugar-beet cultivation is largely carried on in north France, Germany, and south Russia.

The cultivation of the vine is an important European industry, the vine thriving in those warm countries in which wheat can be cultivated. The plant grows best on well-drained slopes, exposed to genial summer heat. The dried grape—in the form of currants and raisins—is largely produced in the drier, eastern Mediterranean peninsulas.

Animals.

Of the wild animals of Europe the reindeer, bear, boar, wolf, and deer are noteworthy. The animals protected and reared by mankind are those supplying food, clothing, and means of transport, viz. sheep, cattle, pigs, and horses.

Fish are very abundant in both the seas and rivers of Europe. In the shallow North Sea and in the shallow coastal submerged plains generally, cod, herring, and other fish are obtained. The swift, cold rivers of the north-west supply salmon; and the warm, sluggish, muddy rivers of the Caspian are fished for sturgeon.

Minerals.

Coal and *iron*. In many parts of Europe there occur in the coal-bearing rocks seams of iron-ore. In the following countries coal and iron-ore are mined, often in the same districts: Great Britain, N. Spain, E. France, Meuse valley, N.W. Germany, S. Germany, Poland, S. and

Vineyards in Germany

Central Russia. In Sweden iron-ores outcrop, but no coal is found near.

Petroleum is pumped from wells in the lowlands lying north-east of the Karpathians in Poland and in Rumania. *Gold* and *platinum* are chiefly produced from the Ural Mts and *silver* in Germany. *Lead* is mined in Spain and Germany. *Copper* mining is important in south-west Spain, and in Sweden. *Zinc* is obtained in Germany and Belgium; and *tin* is produced from mines in south-west England.

Distribution of Population.

In the tundra, and in the high lands of Europe, there are the least number of people to every square mile. The agricultural and pastoral districts support more people, the density of population decreasing to the south-east. It is in the rich mineral districts, and especially on the coalfields, that there are most people to every square mile. For instance, around the Clyde, Mersey, Meuse, lower Rhine, and upper Elbe there are very large populations.

Commercial relations between peoples, supplying each other with commodities which they best produce and receiving in return goods which they cannot produce, tend to gather the population at places conveniently facing their neighbours oversea. London, Rotterdam, Hamburg, and Havre have grown for these reasons.

The British Isles.

Position and Size.

The British Isles consist of about 5000 islands. The largest of these are Great Britain (England, Wales, and Scotland), Ireland, the Shetlands, Orkneys, Outer Hebrides, Inner Hebrides, Isle of Man, Isle of Anglesey,

Isle of Wight, the Channel Islands, and Scilly Isles..
The total area of these islands is over 120,000 square
miles.

Surface and General Features.

The political boundary, separating Great Britain into
Scotland in the north, and England and Wales in the
south, runs from the Solway Firth north-east over a
mountainous country, the Cheviot Hills, to the lower
Tweed.

The country north of the boundary may be divided
into

(i)   a great area of high land, lying north of a line
drawn from the mouth of the R. Clyde to the mouth of
the R. Dee ;

(ii)   a central lowland district, broken into a north-
west and a south-east part by a ridge of hills ;

(iii)   a southern upland region, widest in a S.W.—
N.E. direction.

The Highlands of Scotland are divided by a great
valley, Glenmore, into the Northern and Southern Highlands.   It is to the east of the south-west end of this
valley that Ben Nevis, the greatest height in the British
Isles, reaches 4406 ft.

The surface of England and Wales is very irregular,
and presents a striking contrast to that of Scotland.
Stretching as far south as parallel 53° N., and nearer the
west than the east coast, there is a belt of high land,
the Pennine Chain.   In the north-west of England lies
the Lake District, rising to central peaks from all sides.
In the south-west of England there are several hilly
districts, the chief of which are Dartmoor, Exmoor,
Bodmin Moor, and the Mendip Hills.

The remaining part of England may be considered
as a great plain, crossed by two sets of hills :

(1)   the *Limestone Hills*—Cotswolds, Northampton-
shire and Leicestershire Uplands, Lincoln Heights, and
the Yorkshire Moors ;

Ullswater, in the Lake District

(2) the *Chalk Downs*, extending
  (a) in a S.W.—N.E. direction from the Western
       Downs through Salisbury Plain to the
       White Horse Hills, and Chiltern Hills,
       and then northward through the East
       Anglian Heights and Lincolnshire Wolds
       to the Yorkshire Wolds,
  (b) eastward, to form the North Downs,
  (c) south-easterly, to form the South Downs.

The mountains of Wales (Cambrian Mts) are highest near their western edge. Snowdon in the north-west is the highest peak.

The central part of Ireland is a low plain. North of it lie the Donegal Highlands, Antrim Plateau, and Mourne Mts. Southern Ireland is a very mountainous country and includes the Kerry and Wicklow Mts.

Divides and Rivers.

In England the main divide runs north—south near to meridian 2° W., until it reaches Salisbury Plain, where it branches and runs west—east. This divide is nearer the west than the east coast. Consequently the Eden, Lune, Ribble, Mersey, Warwick Avon, and Bristol Avon are short and swift. The eastward-flowing rivers, Tyne, Wear, Tees, Yorkshire Ouse, Witham, Welland, Nene, Great Ouse, Yare, and Thames are long and slow. Of the rivers flowing southward from the west—east divide, the chief are the Tamar, Exe, and Salisbury Avon.

The divide in Wales runs north—south. From it many short and swift rivers drain to the Irish Sea. Several large rivers are shed eastward. Of these the Dee runs north, while the Severn, Wye, and Usk turn southward.

The three divides of Scotland runs S.W.—N.E. From the south part of the Highlands flow the Spey, Dee, Tay, and Forth. The Clyde runs north-west across the Central Lowlands from the Southern Uplands, which also shed the Tweed east, and the Annan and Nith southward.

In several cases, the Irish rivers rise near the sea,

but follow long courses inland before they empty into
the sea.   The chief Irish rivers are the Shannon, Boyne,
Liffey, Barrow-Nore-Suir, Blackwater, Lee, Foyle, and
Bann.

Lakes.

The greater number of the British lakes are flooded
portions of river valleys.   Such lakes are to be found in
the Highlands of Scotland, in the Lake District, and
in Kerry.   In central and north-east Ireland there are
many large, shallow lakes.

The Coasts and Seas of the British Isles.

Headlands, promontories, or capes are to be found
where the Northern Highlands, Mts of Kerry, Welsh
Mts, Wicklow Mts, Cornwall and Devon Moors, the Lake
District, Yorkshire Moors, Southern Uplands, and the
Chalk Downs reach the sea.   Very shallow areas occur
as continuations of the inland plains, as in the Central
Lowlands of Scotland, the Central Plain of Ireland, and
the Lancashire and Cheshire Plain.

Where the rivers enter the seas they tend to deposit
their suspended matter, so forming shallow areas, such
as the Firths of Tay and Forth, the Humber, Thames,
Severn, and Shannon mouths.   In some cases there
appear to be signs that valleys running seawards have
been partly submerged, as in S.W. Ireland and N.W.
Scotland.

Of the straits separating the islands of the United
Kingdom, the North Channel is the deepest, while St
George's Channel is a large submerged valley widening
and deepening to the south and west.   The English
Channel is shallow, especially so in the Strait of Dover.
The North Sea is shallow, and only deepens in the
extreme north.   Between Great Britain and Europe,
about latitude 55° N., there is a very shallow area, the
Dogger Bank.

Climate of the British Isles.

(a) Air-temperatures.

Air-temperatures in the British Isles increase from north to south. Over land the air is hot in summer, but over the sea (in the same latitude) the air is only warm. In winter the air over the land is cold, while that over the sea is cool. As the prevailing winds of the British Isles blow from the west and south-west they bring warm air inland in summer; and so at this time of the year the air-temperatures are lower in the west of our isles than in the east. In winter, cool air drifts over land from the western seas, and this air becomes colder during its passage inland; thus in winter the air-temperatures decrease from west to east. In the west of the British Isles the range in air-temperatures is therefore less than the range in the east.

(b) Rainfall.

The prevailing winds of these islands cool as they go northward. This cooling causes the air to hold less water vapour, and the excess of vapour condenses to tiny drops of liquid water. Further cooling causes the drops to increase in size and in weight to such an extent that they fall to earth as rain. The rainfall decreases in amount in a north-easterly direction.

The upward movement of the air, where it has to pass over mountainous country, also causes cooling of the air and the condensation of some of the water vapour. Generally, the windward sides of the British hilly districts receive more rain than the lee sides.

The plants and animals of the British Isles.

With sufficient rain, and fairly equable air-temperatures, the British Isles are naturally fitted for the growth of trees, except in the elevated districts of north Scotland, north-west and south-west Ireland, Wales, and the Pennines. In the north of Britain the greater number of trees are conifers; and in south Britain the

deciduous trees are more abundant than conifers. The
highlands and uplands of the British Isles are either
moorland or waste land. The lower slopes of the hills
are poor grass lands, and in the wetter plains there are
rich meadow lands.

A Red Deer

The native animals, bears, beavers, boars, and wolves,
have been completely destroyed by mankind during the
last 2000 years. Besides the wild deer (red and fallow),
smaller wild animals such as the fox, badger, wild cat,
weasel, otter, squirrel, hare, rabbit, and rat still exist.

Pasture and Agriculture.

One-third of the surface of the British Isles is under permanent pasture. In the highlands and uplands little or no attempt is made to produce any crops, and sheep are allowed to feed on the poor grasses. Thus sheep-rearing is very important in the Southern Uplands, in Wales, and on the Limestone Hills and Chalk Downs; and these pastures support nearly four million sheep.

The wetter plains of Ireland, central Scotland, central and south-west England are rich meadow lands, on which cattle are reared in large numbers. From these districts, which support nearly five million cattle, there come large supplies of dairy produce.

A quarter of the surface of the United Kingdom is arable land. Generally the lowlands provide the land most suitable for cultivation. The wetter parts of these are mostly kept under grass, while the eastern, drier lowlands are cultivated with cereals. In the warm, dry lands west, south, and east of the Wash, wheat is cultivated. Barley is the more important crop in the cooler lands to the north; and oats are largely produced in the colder lowlands of central Scotland.

In certain lowlands which have rich soils large orchards are cultivated, and from these apples, pears, plums, and other fruits are gathered. Such fruit-growing districts are to be found in Devon, Hereford, Gloucester, Worcester, Kent, Essex, Cambridge, and in the Carse of Gowrie, south-east of the Sidlaw Hills.

Hops are grown in south-east England and in Worcestershire; and flax in north-east Ireland.

Fisheries.

In the shallow waters near the coasts, and especially east of the Tyne above the Dogger Bank, fish are very abundant. In addition to cod and herring, there are many flat-fish. Annually the south coasts are visited by mackerel and pilchards. In the swift, cold rivers, especially of the mountainous north of Scotland and north-west of Ireland, salmon are caught.

Of the 'shell-fish,' the oyster is the most important. Oyster-beds are cultivated in the muddy estuaries of the Thames and Essex rivers (near Whitstable and Colchester), the Humber (near Grimsby), and other rivers. The fisheries of the United Kingdom are valued at over £20,000,000 annually, and they employ 100,000 people.

Minerals of the British Isles.

Coal. In Ireland coal is not abundant. The only important coalfield lies between the rivers Nore and Barrow in north-east County Kilkenny.

Scotland is more fortunate in its coal supplies. These lie in the Central Lowlands. The area under which workable coal seams lie stretches from the west coast in Ayrshire to the south-east coast of Fifeshire.

The greatest area of the British coalfields occurs in England. The chief district in which coal is worked lies east, south, and west of the Pennine Chain. The leading coalfields are:

(i)   Northumberland—Durham.
(ii)   West Riding of Yorkshire, Nottingham-
        shire and E. Derbyshire.
(iii)   West Cumberland.
(iv)   South Lancashire.
(v)   North Staffordshire.
(vi)   South Staffordshire.
(vii)   Coalbrookdale.
(viii) East Warwickshire.
(ix)   Leicestershire.
(x)   Bristol.

In Wales, there are two large coalfields, (*a*) Denbighshire and Flintshire, (*b*) South Wales.

Iron. The chief iron-mining districts are not on the coalfields but near to them. In north-east Yorkshire, between the mouth of the Tees and the Cleveland Hills, there are large deposits of 'Cleveland ironstone'; and the amount produced is about half the total iron-ore raised in the British Isles. Almost opposite to

Cleveland lies the busy iron-mining and smelting district known as Furness. There are several iron-mining districts near the Limestone Hills, particularly at Frodingham in north Lincolnshire. In Scotland there are local supplies of iron-ore on the coalfields. In Ireland the only iron-ore district is in Antrim.

Salt is largely mined in Cheshire, and north of the mouth of the Tees. Building stones are generally abundant. *Granite* is quarried in Aberdeenshire, on

Splitting and dressing slates at a Welsh quarry

Dartmoor, in Leicestershire, and in the Mourne Mts. *Slates* are quarried in north Wales, near Snowdon, and exported from Bangor and Carnarvon. *Limestone* is obtained from parts of the Pennine Chain, and from the Limestone Hills. In the granite areas of Devon and Cornwall, deposits of *kaolin*, a grey clay produced by the weathering and decomposition of granite, are worked for exportation to the north Staffordshire potteries, Other minerals mined in the British Isles are *copper*, *zinc*, *lead*, and *tin*. *Oil* has recently been discovered, by sinking bore-holes in Derbyshire and elsewhere.

People, race, and religion.

The United Kingdom is peopled by Teutons and Normans, except in the north and west, where the older Celtic race is found. Many Celts live in Scotland, the Isle of Man, Wales, and Ireland. Owing to trade and other reasons there are large numbers of foreigners living in our islands, chiefly at the ports facing the continent of Europe. Nearly half a million British people emigrate each year, the percentage from Ireland and Scotland being very large.

All forms of religion are fully tolerated in the United Kingdom, the Protestant forms of worship being more prevalent in Great Britain, and the Roman Catholic form of worship being professed by three-fourths of the population of Ireland. Elementary education is compulsory and free. Secondary schools, technical schools, and colleges are increasing in number. There are universities in England at Oxford, Cambridge, Durham, London, Birmingham, Manchester, Liverpool, Leeds, Sheffield and Bristol; in Wales, at Aberystwyth, Bangor, and Cardiff; in Scotland, at Aberdeen, Edinburgh, Glasgow, and St Andrews ; and in Ireland there are the University of Dublin, the National University of Ireland (Cork, Dublin, and Galway), and Queen's University, Belfast.

Population and its distribution.

In 1911 the people of the British Isles numbered over 45 millions. England and Wales had a population of 36, Scotland nearly 5, and Ireland over 4 millions. In the other islands, there were over one-tenth million people. So, with an area of over 120,000 sq. mls., the average population of the British Isles was about 370 people to every square mile.

The distribution of this huge population is very uneven. The varying altitudes of the land, the varying fertility of the soil, and the distribution of the minerals all affect the density of the population.

The Industries of the British Isles.

The majority of the people of the British Isles at one time were farmers. The fairs, or holidays, of the people soon became opportunities for doing business; and in many towns there are still held cattle, sheep, horse, and other fairs, to which farmers and traders come from all parts.

With the discovery and working of our minerals, and the invention of all kinds of machinery, manufacturing industries are now more important than either agriculture or pasture. Ireland, Scotland with the exception of its central manufacturing district, central and north Wales, and south, east, and the hilly regions of England are the chief agricultural and pastoral districts.

Industries dependent on Agriculture and Pasture.

A century ago the chief iron goods made in the British Isles were for use on farms. Agricultural implements are now made at the 'fair' towns. Pig-iron is brought from the iron-smelting districts, and it is then cast, or wrought, into ploughs, harrows, and other implements. Important agricultural-implement works are to be found at Grantham, Lincoln, Ipswich, and Bedford.

Flour milling centres have arisen wherever windmills could be profitably erected in grain-producing districts, and also where water power was available for watermills. Associated with these flour-producing districts there are large biscuit factories, such as those of Reading, Carlisle, and Edinburgh. Breweries, dependent on supplies of barley, hops, and good water, have long been in existence in nearly every market town. The breweries of Burton, London, and Dublin, are noted throughout the kingdom.

In grazing districts the large supplies of hides support leather industries. Thus the East Anglian plains have given rise to the Norwich boot and shoe trade; the plains between the Limestone Hills and the

Chalk Downs have developed Northampton and the neighbouring towns of Kettering, Wellingborough, and Leicester into leather-working centres. Similarly, between the Pennines and the Limestone Hills, the rich grazing lands support leather industries at Stafford and elsewhere. It is interesting to note here that the large supply of hides from the cattle imported to the London docks has created, in the Bermondsey district of South London, a large leather-tanning industry.

The fruit-growing districts of south-west and south-east England, and of the Carse of Gowrie, have given rise to jam industries at London and Dundee; and to cider and other industries in Devonshire and Herefordshire.

The Coal Industry.

Over one million out of the forty-five million people of the United Kingdom are engaged in coal-mining. Many other people are occupied in transporting and selling the coal, and large towns exist in which this is the chief trade. The six large coalfields which reach to the seas are the most important for trade in coal. Large amounts of coal are now sent by rail, especially to London, from the near coalfields, such as the East Warwickshire and the Leicestershire coalfields. But the chief coal supplies are used on the coalfields for steam-raising and metal-smelting purposes.

The Iron Industry.

The occurrence of beds of iron-ore in the coal-bearing rocks of the coalfields has been known from early times, and Sheffield and Birmingham have been iron-working districts for centuries. The working of these local supplies of ore has started large iron industries, which now are supported by foreign ores and by the Cleveland and Furness ores.

For iron goods generally, or hardware, the South Staffordshire coalfield has long been noted. Birmingham,

Wolverhampton, Wednesbury, Walsall, and other large towns lie in this 'Black Country. On the Clyde and Forth coalfield great ironworks, chiefly fed by foreign ores, are to be found at Glasgow, Airdrie, and Falkirk. In south Wales, especially near Merthyr, there are large ironworks—most of the ore here smelted coming from Spain. At Swansea and the neighbouring towns steel plates are coated with tin. Here also copper ore is smelted. Cleveland ore is smelted at Middlesbrough, and the Furness ore at Barrow-in-Furness. Both districts are dependent on imported coal, as they have *no* local supplies. Some of the Furness ore is taken to the west Cumberland coal ports for smelting and working.

A Belfast Shipyard

The greatest iron industry is that connected with the production of steel. Sheffield, the second largest town in Yorkshire, is famous throughout the world for its steel goods. Cutlery was originally the chief product, the local supplies of hard, gritty sandstone being found exceptionally good for grindstones. The finest steel goods of all kinds are now made at this city, which is built where the Sheaf runs northward into the Don. A large amount of Swedish pig-iron is imported up the Don to supply the Sheffield forges. Warrington, at the head of the Mersey estuary, produces steel wire.

The ship-building industry is very closely connected with the iron industry, and may be considered as part of it. The Clyde estuary is the most important ship-building district in the world, receiving coal and iron from the coalfield to the south-east. The large towns engaged in ship-building are Glasgow, Port Glasgow, and Greenock. The lower Tyne, running east through the Northumberland-Durham coalfield, is another great ship-building district. Newcastle, Gateshead, and Jarrow are its chief centres. There is a similar industry at Barrow-in-Furness. Belfast, in north-east Ireland, at the head of Belfast Lough, is a very important ship-building town, at which some of the largest merchant ships afloat have been built. Both coal and iron, however, must be imported in large amounts to Belfast from the opposite coasts of Great Britain.

Textile Industries.

(a) The Woollen Industry.

There are small woollen industries in the Tweed valley, chiefly at the towns of Hawick and Galashiels; in the valleys west and south of the Cotswolds—at Stroud (Frome valley), Bradford (Avon valley), and Frome (Frome valley, Somersetshire); and in the Severn valley, in mid-Wales at Welshpool and other towns. The wool used in these districts is largely obtained from local pastures, and part of the power for driving the machinery comes from the swiftly flowing rivers.

The use of the steam-engine and the need for coal supplies have developed the woollen industry to its greatest extent in the valleys of the Aire and Calder, in the north of the West Riding coalfield. The important towns in this district are Leeds and Bradford in the

Aire basin, and Halifax, Huddersfield, Dewsbury, and Wakefield in the Calder basin. Leicester, in the valley of the Soar, a south-bank tributary of the Trent, has a woollen hosiery industry. On the east part of the Scottish coalfield at Bannockburn, and also at Kilmarnock on the Ayrshire coalfield, there are woollen industries.

Large supplies of wool are imported from the grass regions of South America, Australia, and New Zealand to London. From the metropolis the wool is sent to the manufacturing districts by rail.

(b)   The Cotton Industry.

The supply of raw cotton from the south-east of the United States of America attracted the cotton industry to the west of Great Britain. The damp atmosphere west of the Pennine Chain and the water-power obtainable from the swift streams led to the erection of cotton mills in south Lancashire. The local coalfield provides cheap fuel for the steam-power which is now used in place of water-power.

The rivers running south from the Lancashire Moors and west from the Pennines unite in the Irwell, a north-bank tributary of the Mersey. The Irwell-Mersey basin is the greatest cotton-spinning district in the world. The large cotton-spinning towns, built near the hills and on the rivers, are Bolton, Bury, Rochdale, Oldham, Ashton, and Stockport. The city of Manchester, situated on the Irwell at the meeting-place of routes from the above-named towns, is the great warehouse for the manufactured goods of the cotton mills. A great amount of raw cotton is imported through Liverpool; but some is taken up the Manchester Ship Canal direct to Manchester.

On the north side of the Lancashire Moors the valleys of the lower Ribble, and of its tributaries the Colne and Calder, have a very damp climate, and also water and coal-power. These conditions have led to the growth of the large cotton-weaving towns of Preston, Blackburn, Burnley, and Accrington.

West of the Clyde a coal district with the necessary

damp climate has developed cotton industries at Paisley, where much sewing-cotton is manufactured.

Lace and lace-goods are manufactured at Nottingham on the Trent.

(c) **The Linen Industry.**

In the cool, moist climate of the north of our islands flax can be grown. The linen industry has grown up in these districts, especially in Ulster, at Belfast, Londonderry, and other towns. The coal needed for this industry is imported from Great Britain. The coalfield of south Fifeshire has helped to develop the linen trade at Dunfermline. Flax, obtained from the Baltic lands, is imported to the Forth and Tay estuaries for the Scottish linen industry.

(d) **Other textile industries.**

From the Baltic lands hemp is imported to the Scottish linen districts; and from the tropical delta of the Ganges jute is imported to Dundee. The coarse textiles manufactured from jute and hemp are sail-cloth, canvas, and ropes, and these are made chiefly at Dundee.

The Huguenot refugees from France, who came to London in 1685, were silk-weavers; and they settled at Spitalfields, there carrying on the silk industry. This industry later spread to the district west and east of the south end of the Pennines, where large supplies of suitable water are available. Macclesfield and Congleton on the east Cheshire coalfield, and Chesterfield and Derby on the Derbyshire coalfield, are the chief places where silk goods are made. Silk goods are also made at Dublin, Glasgow, and Bradford (Yorks.).

Other industries.

The coal seams of north Staffordshire outcrop among a series of very fine clays. Here large pottery works have grown up around the source of the Trent, and this district is known throughout the kingdom as the 'Potteries.' The large, inseparable towns of Tunstall, Burslem, Hanley, Stoke, Fenton, and Longton are now

Jute warehouse, Dundee

united under the name of Stoke-on-Trent, with a population of nearly 250,000 people.

From the salt of Cheshire and of the mouth of the
Tees—both near to coalfields—large chemical industries
have sprung up. St Helens, Widnes, and Runcorn are
fed by the Cheshire mines; and Newcastle by the
Durham mines. Large 'table salt' industries also exist
on the saltfields at Northwich, Middlewich, and Nant-
wich, and near to Stockton-on-Tees.

A minor industry is the hat trade. Men's felt hats
are made at Denton, near Manchester, and men's 'straw'
hats at Luton, Bedfordshire. Luton also manufactures
the greater number of ladies' 'straw' hats. Most of the
plait used in this industry is imported from Japan.

Position of Towns.

Some of the oldest towns in the British Isles have
grown up around castles. Many of these castles were
built on prominent hills commanding valley routes (e.g.
Chester, Kilkenny); and especially where rivers had cut
gaps (defiles, or gorges) through hills (e.g. Perth, Lincoln).
The junction of valley routes (e.g. Reading, Sheffield),
the presence of fords across rivers (e.g. Bedford) or of
bridges over rivers (e.g. London), the limit of navigation
of a river (e.g. York), were other causes for the growth
of towns. The water power of the rivers flowing from
the Pennine Chain, Welsh Mts, Cotswolds, and Southern
Uplands led to the growth of industrial centres; and
suitable water-supply determined the sites of Burton-
on-Trent, the silk-weaving towns south of the Pennines,
and various inland watering places (e.g. Bath, Harrogate).
Ports have grown along the shores of navigable estuaries,
and packet stations have been established where suitable
harbours existed, or could be constructed, near to the
Continental and Irish shores (e.g. Dover, Harwich,
Holyhead, Kingston). Many large towns have been built
along the coast, either for residential purposes or as
holiday resorts, their sites often having been chosen
because of the natural beauty of the local scenery
(e.g. Bournemouth).

Internal Communications.

Valleys, and saddles leading over hills from one valley to another, have long been natural routes into the interior of Great Britain and Ireland. The rivers themselves, and roads where the rivers were not navigable, provided the means of communication. In more recent times canals have been constructed where rivers were not navigable, and not a few of these canals have been constructed over saddles and divides. Canals are especially suited for the transport of non-perishable goods; hence their development in the 'mineral areas.' The chief British canal is the Manchester Ship Canal, which runs from the south side of the Mersey estuary, partly along the R. Mersey, and then partly along the R. Irwell to Manchester. From this city vessels sail down the canal to all parts of the world.

Railways.

The practical developments of the locomotive and of the railway, within the last century, have altered communication entirely. Between the large towns of the British Isles railways have been constructed, chiefly along valleys, and especially through gaps and over saddles, in order to avoid steep gradients.

London is the starting point of most of the railways of England. These railways have been constructed in all directions, their names generally indicating the direction taken from London.

The chief railways of England are:
  (i)   Great Northern.
  (ii)   Midland.
  (iii) London and North-Western.
  (iv)   Great Central.
  (v)   Great Western.
  (vi)   London and South-Western.
  (vii) London, Brighton, and South Coast.
  (viii) South-Eastern and Chatham.
  (ix)   Great Eastern.
  (x)   Lancashire and Yorkshire.
  (xi)   North-Eastern.

Wales is served by the English lines (iii) and (v), and by the Cambrian railway.

In Scotland the chief railways, which are all in connection with the English lines, are :
  (i)   North British.
  (ii) Caledonian.
  (iii) Glasgow and South-Western.
  (iv) Highland.
  (v)   Great North of Scotland.

The leading Irish railways start at Dublin, and their names indicate their direction from that city. These are:
  (i)   Great Northern (Ireland).
  (ii) Midland Great Western.
  (iii) Great Southern and Western.
  (iv) Dublin and South-Eastern.

The Commerce of the United Kingdom.

The following table shows the value, in millions of pounds sterling, of the goods imported into and exported from the British Isles.

Class	Imports		Exports	
	1918	1919	1918	1919
Food, Drink, and Tobacco ...	570	712	16	76
Raw Materials	458	647	75	212
Manufactured Articles	280	267	419	663
Miscellaneous Goods	8	6	22	12
Total Value (Millions sterling)	1316	1632	532	963

The chief exports from the British Isles (in order of value) are coal, cotton and woollen goods, and iron and steel goods. In 1919, a half (in value) of our exports went to Central and Western Europe, mainly to those nations who were our Allies during the War.

A third (in value) of our imports comes from our colonies, and nearly a half comes from the United States of America and South America. The sources from which our food supplies came in 1913 and in 1918 are shown below; the amount received from each source is stated as a percentage of the total, and the total shows the weight in thousands of tons.

Source of Supply	Wheat and Flour		Meat (excluding Bacon and Hams)		Bacon and Hams		Sugar		Dairy Produce	
	1913	1918	1913	1918	1913	1918	1913	1918	1913	1918
	%	%	%	%	%	%	%	%	%	%
Europe	5·0	—	6·2	—	49·0	0·2	76·8	1·1	74·6	12·6
U.S.A.	34·7	52·3	1·6	31·2	44·9	83·7	0·2	0·4	0·2	37·8
Canada	22·5	25·1	0·1	5·0	5·8	15·2	—	—	10·4	20·6
S. America	12·9	15·5	54·9	38·4	—	—	1·7	3·8	0·6	4·5
Australasia	8·7	4·6	36·5	22·5	—	—	—	—	11·3	22·2
Other Countries	16·2	2·5	0·7	2·9	0·3	0·9	21·3	94·7	2·9	2·3
Total (weight in thousands of tons)	6126	4632	878	660	286	601	1969	1306	621	360

About 10 % of our wheat and flour supply in 1913 came from India. Nearly all the sugar imported during 1918 came from Cuba, Java, and Mauritius.

East Coast Ports.

Aberdeen has exports of granite, and is visited by ships from London, and also from Norway and the Baltic. *Dundee* and *Kirkcaldy* receive fibres from the Baltic and from India for their coarse textiles trade. *Leith* and *Grangemouth* export various minerals and manufactured goods. Leith trades with Scandinavia, the Baltic, and Germany, importing much timber and wood-pulp for the paper trade of Edinburgh. *Newcastle* and the Tyne ports east of it, together with *Sunderland,* have exporting trade in coal, and in iron goods; and they receive timber, iron, and other goods from Europe. *Hull* is due east of the Aire valley, and nearly due east of Preston and Leeds. It exports much coal, and also cotton and woollen goods from the mills of Lancashire and Yorkshire. There is great trade from this port with the Baltic, Germany, the Netherlands, the Mediterranean, and East Indies.   Hull has large imports of grain, wool, and timber.

South-east of Hull, on the south bank of the Humber, the new port of *Immingham* has been made for the great coal trade of Doncaster and the Don valley, and for the exports of Sheffield and Rotherham.   Only a few miles south-east of Immingham lies the port of *Grimsby*, which, along with *Yarmouth*, receives large supplies of cod, herring, and other Dogger Bank fish for transit to London.   *Harwich* is the packet-station for the Hook of Holland, Rotterdam, Antwerp, and Hamburg.

The Port of London.

From the time of the Romans, who built a bridge across the Thames, all large ships have been compelled to anchor east of the bridge.   At first embankments were built around the Thames on which the imported goods were landed; and some of these have now been replaced by docks cut out of the soft and easily-excavated sediments which the Thames has deposited along its banks. To these docks come ships from Australasia, India, and the Far East, the Union of South Africa, the United States of America, and South America.   Such goods as grain, wood, wool, wine, tea, meat (live and dead) are imported to these docks; and, in return for these commodities, manufactured goods of every description are sent from the British manufacturing districts for exportation.

From *Tilbury* docks large liners start for the Cape of Good Hope, Asia, and Australasia.   The packet-station of *Queenborough*, east of the mouth of the Medway, connects with the Netherlands packet-station of Flushing.

South Coast Ports.

Dover, Folkestone, Newhaven, and *Southampton* are packet-stations for Flushing, Ostend, Calais, Boulogne, Dieppe, Havre, and the Channel Islands.   Southampton is becoming a great port for America, and from it sail the mail boats for the Cape. *Portsmouth* is a great

The Royal Victoria Docks, London

naval station. *Portland* is also an important naval station. *Plymouth—Devonport*, a large naval dockyard, is a port of call for Atlantic liners, and for Irish packet and trading steamers.

West Coast Ports.

Bristol, some miles from the mouth of the Avon, trades with Ireland and with America. Its new outport of *Avonmouth* is able to dock very large steamers. Large quantities of tobacco, sugar, and cacao are imported to Bristol's tobacco and cocoa factories. *Cardiff*, the port of Wales, is the third port of the British Isles. The chief exports are coal and the metal goods manufactured on the South Wales coalfield. Irish provisions and dairy produce are largely imported to feed the dense population of the neighbouring coalfield. *Swansea* receives iron and copper-ore from Spain, and tin from the Federated Malay States and elsewhere, and exports manufactured goods. *Fishguard*, on a bay looking north into Cardigan Bay, is the Great Western Railway Co.'s packet-station, from which steamers run to *Rosslare*, the outport of Wexford. *Holyhead*, on the north shore of Holyhead I. which lies west of Anglesey, is the London and North-Western Railway Co.'s packet-station for Dublin and Greenore. *Liverpool* (with its extension over the Mersey estuary at Birkenhead) is the second port of Great Britain, and the chief port for trade with America, and with Africa and Ireland. Cotton, grain, provisions, timber, meat, wool are typical imports. The chief exports are manufactured goods, such as woollens, cottons, and iron goods. Large numbers of people emigrate from this port to America. The ports on the east coast of Ireland, *Belfast, Drogheda, Dundalk, Dublin*, and *Wexford*, trade very largely with Liverpool. The American liners which leave Liverpool call at *Queenstown*, the outport of *Cork*, for Irish passengers. *Whitehaven*, on the west shore of the Lake District, is a coal-port, supplying coal to the linen-manufacturing towns of Ulster. *Stranraer* is the nearest packet-station to the Irish coast; it trades with *Larne*, the packet-station of Belfast.

Glasgow and other large towns in the Clyde estuary are engaged both in foreign and in coastal trade. The Atlantic steamers leaving the Clyde call at *Moville*, at the north end of Lough Foyle. *Greenock*, at the mouth of the Clyde, has sugar-refineries. *Oban*, at the south end of Glenmore, is a small packet-station and tourist centre.

Government and Administration.

Our government is a limited monarchy. The present monarch, King George V, succeeded to the throne on the 6th of May, 1910. The power of the monarch is practically wielded by a Cabinet, containing the Prime Minister and about 20 other Ministers, who are chosen from the political party in majority in the House of Commons. This House is composed of 707 members, who represent cities and boroughs, counties, and a few universities. The House of Lords consists of Peers who have inherited the right to take a share in the government, of Peers created by the King, of some English Bishops, of Irish Peers elected for life, and of Scottish Peers elected to sit for each parliament.

France.

Position and Size.

France is our nearest continental neighbour, being separated from Great Britain by the Straits of Dover, which widens westward to the English Channel. The sea also forms the boundary of France on the west and in the south-east. Belgium in the north, Germany, Switzerland, and Italy to the east, and Spain to the south, are its other neighbours. Its area is nearly twice that of the British Isles.

The Mer de Glace, Mont Blanc

Surface and General Features.

A line drawn from the south point of the west coast in a north-easterly direction separates France into a northerly lowland and a southerly highland district. Hilly districts are to be found, however, in the Brittany peninsula, which runs west to the Atlantic. As we go south-east, the land gradually rises to a height of over 5000 feet above the sea. The higher part of this south-east district forms the Central plateau. From the high, eastern edge of this plateau there is a very steep descent to the Rhone valley. The Central plateau continues north-east, becoming narrower, and being known as the Langres plateau. The Vosges Mts lie to the east of this plateau; eastward of the Vosges Mts, French territory now extends as far as the Rhine. From the Vosges, going south, we pass over a low saddle, and then over the S.W.—N.E. Jura Mts, which fall steeply southward to the upper Rhone valley. South and east of the Rhone lie the Alps, which continue southward to the Mediterranean coast. Their highest peak in the north-west is Mont Blanc (15,776 ft.). Separated from the Central plateau by a low saddle, the Pyrenees form a natural boundary between France and Spain. North of the Langres plateau, but separated from it by an area of lowland, the wooded plateau of the Ardennes continues from France into Belgium and Germany.

Divides and Rivers.

The chief divide of France runs north-east, from about the middle of the Pyrenees. The rivers flowing north and west are the Meuse, Seine, Loire, Dordogne-Garonne. The Saône-Rhone is the only important river flowing southward. The Rhone and many parallel streams run west from the Alps into the Saône, bringing much water and suspended matter, and helping to make the Saône-Rhone very swift. Alsace-Lorraine is in the Rhine basin; this area is drained chiefly by the Moselle and the Saar.

Coasts.

On the north coast, opposite to England, the chalk rocks form the headland of Cape Gris-Nez. Further west Cape de la Hague and the Ushant promontory project into the Atlantic Ocean. The Bay of Biscay forms the western boundary of the country. The Mediterranean coast, from the Pyrenees to the Rhone delta, has been so much silted up by the Rhone sediments that the only good harbours lie east of the Rhone in the rocky coast of the Maritime Alps. The island of Corsica, which lies south-east of this coast, belongs to France.

Climate.

Nearly all France lies south of the British Isles, and consequently its air-temperatures are higher than those of England. The average air-temperatures increase generally as we go southward. The eastward indraught of air from the Atlantic Ocean modifies the normal air-temperatures, so that the coastal lands have warm winters and cool summers, while the country further east has normal cold winters and hot summers.

The western lowlands of France receive a plentiful supply of rain. The rainfall gradually diminishes as we go south-east. On the Mediterranean coast, and in the lower Rhone valley, the north winds give little rain in summer. This coastal strip has less than 1 inch of rain in July. At Marseilles the rainfall in June, July, and August is about 1 inch, 0·5 inch, and 1 inch respectively. [Compare Paris, with a rainfall of about 2 inches in each of these months.]

Plants and Animals.

Woods of deciduous trees are still extensive in the uplands, being replaced by coniferous trees in the highlands; forests of silver fir are extensive on the slopes of the Vosges. In the very high parts of the Alps trees will not grow. The wooded and waste mountainous regions are still the haunts of wolves and bears, which are largely protected for sport.

Agriculture.

Barley is grown in the north, wheat in the central lowlands of the Seine and Loire basins, and maize in the warmer Garonne valley. Flax is largely grown in northern France, and the sugar-beet is very important in all the northern parts. South of a line running north-east from near the mouth of the Loire the vine is cultivated extensively, especially in the higher parts of the Seine, Loire, Dordogne-Garonne, and the Saône-Rhone valleys. The south and south-east parts of France have the Mediterranean type of vegetation. Olives around the Gulf of the Lion, the mulberry tree in the lower Rhone valley, and fruits such as the lemon form very valuable groves. Vineyards and hop-gardens are cultivated in Alsace, where wheat and barley are also grown.

Lowland cattle pastures are extensive in the wet west, while in the uplands and highlands sheep are pastured.

Fisheries.

There are small fishing ports round the coasts of France, the chief being Dunkirk and Nantes. There are also fishing grounds off the coasts of Normandy and Brittany. On the south-east coast of the Mediterranean there are small tunny fisheries.

Minerals.

Coal. The three important French coalfields are:—

(i) Northern, stretching from the Pas de Calais east-ward between the valleys of the Lys and Escaut (Scheldt) towards the Sambre valley. (Pre-war production, 30 million tons annually).

(ii) South-eastern, near St Etienne and Le Creuzot. (Pre-war production, 10 million tons annually).

(iii) Saar, lying east of Metz, mainly along the Saar valley. (Pre-war production, 12 million tons annually.) The mines of this district have been ceded to France, as compensation for the damage which the Germans did to the coal mines in the northern coalfield.

Iron-ore. 95 % of the iron-ore is raised in the Moselle basin, in the triangle between Longwy (near the Belgium-Luxemburg frontier), Thionville (on the Moselle), and Nancy (on the Meurthe). *Briey* is the centre of the most productive mines. By the restoration of Lorraine to France, Germany loses annually over 20 million tons of iron-ore (three quarters of her pre-war annual production).

Building stones, clays, and other earthy minerals are abundant in the hilly districts. From the gypsum, occurring in the rocks near Paris, 'plaster of Paris' is made.

People.

The Celts of Brittany, Gauls of the plains, and the Iberians of the Garonne and Mediterranean coast were in early times conquered by the Romans, whose Latin tongue they learned. Later, France was overrun by Teutonic tribes, especially by the Franks, from whom the country has gained its name. Thus the population at present is very mixed. The northern people are of tall stature, with light eyes and hair, while the southern people are smaller, with dark eyes and hair. Education is free and compulsory, and similar to that in the British Isles. The majority of French people are Roman Catholics.

The population numbers over 41 millions, much less than that of the British Isles, though France is nearly twice the size.

Industries.

The French are more of an agricultural nation than are the British, 44 % of the working population being occupied in agriculture. The greatest agricultural (or rather horticultural) product is the vine, there being over one and a half million vine-growers in France. Wine-making is a very large industry, especially in the districts of Champagne (upper Seine basin), Burgundy (upper Saône), down the Rhone to the Mediterranean; and in Alsace. In the lower Garonne there is a large claret industry around Bordeaux. The sugar-beet industry is very important, especially in north France.

Sèvres pottery

The Mediterranean climate has helped in the development of the olive oil industry in the lower Rhone, and the natural growth of mulberry trees has encouraged the rearing of silkworms. Over four tons of eggs are incubated yearly, and large amounts of silk are produced locally, more than 100,000 people being employed in silk-culture. And yet silk has to be imported from other countries to supply the great silk factories of Lyons and its neighbour, the coal-mining town of St Etienne.

Woollen and linen industries have grown up around the northern coalfield. Much wool is imported from South America for the industry at Lille and Roubaix. Locally produced flax is still used in the linen trade of Lille and Valenciennes. Cotton industries are also important, the raw cotton being largely imported to Rouen. Lille, Roubaix, Rouen, and Mulhouse are the chief towns where cotton goods are made.

Iron goods are made on the coalfields at Lille, St Etienne, and Le Creuzot. The smelting of iron-ore is an important industry at Nancy, Thionville, and throughout the iron-mining district. Porcelain and pottery are made at Limoges and at Sèvres near Paris.

Communications.

The roads of France are everywhere good. The low divides between the western parts of the Seine, Loire, and Garonne basins all help to make communication easy. Similarly, canal construction has been made easy, especially in the north; and all the large rivers of France are connected by canals. Many of the rivers have been deepened, and provide excellent waterways into the interior plateaux.

The railways radiate from Paris, and they serve all parts of France.

Commerce and Ports.

The chief exports from France are woollen and silk goods, and wine. The chief imports are wool, silk, cotton, and coal. A half of the imports are raw materials, and over half the exports are manufactured goods. The British are the best customers of France.

Calais, Boulogne, and *Dieppe* are packet-stations. *Havre* is a large port, with much American trade. *Dunkirk* is an important commercial port, as also is *St Nazaire,* the outport of Nantes. *Bordeaux* is the chief port for the export of French wines. *Marseilles* is the greatest port of the country, trading with all Mediterranean ports, and via the Suez Canal with Asiatic and Australian ports.

Administration and Towns.

The republic of France is governed by a Chamber of Deputies and a Senate, who together elect a President to hold office for seven years.

Paris (population nearly three millions) is the capital.

It has all kinds of industries, but chiefly those connected with apparel. *Marseilles* is the chief seaport, and the centre of a large soap and oil-refining trade. *Lyons* is the largest silk-manufacturing centre in the world. *Bordeaux* is the wine port of France. *Lille* is also a famous textile centre. *Toulouse* lies in the centre of a rich agricultural belt. *St Etienne* has hardware and silk trade. *Nice* is a winter holiday resort on the Riviera. *Strassburg* and *Metz* are the chief towns of Alsace and of Lorraine respectively.

Belgium.

Position and Size.

Belgium lies to the north of France and east of the North Sea. Holland lies north and Germany east of it. Its area is less than one-tenth of the area of the British Isles.

Surface and General Features.

Belgium slopes gradually north-west to the Rhine. In the south-east the wooded Ardennes plateau rises to a height of 2000 ft. The western part of this country is drained by the Scheldt. In the east the Meuse and its tributary the Sambre flow northward to the Rhine. The soil is generally sandy, especially on the short coast-line of 42 miles.

Climate.

The air-temperatures of the lower part of Belgium vary only slightly from north to south. The high land of the Ardennes, however, produces lower temperatures all the year round. The prevailing winds are similar to those of the British Isles, and rain falls fairly equally over the country. The influence of the eastward-moving air extends throughout the country, causing generally cool winters and warm summers.

Natural Productions.

South-east Belgium is wooded, and in these woods deer and boars run wild. On the poorer hill-pastures at

A Belgian milk-seller with dog-cart

the foot of the Ardennes sheep are reared. The low coastal province of Flanders is noted for its horses.

In the intervening lowlands agriculture is carried on with the greatest care. Oats, rye, wheat, potatoes, and sugar-beet are cultivated, the largest area being under rye and oats, and the least, though most productive, under beet. Cod and herring are the chief fish caught in the North Sea.

Coal is the chief mineral. The Belgian coalfield is a continuation of the French coalfield, and it extends from the middle of the French border along the Sambre, the left-bank tributary of the Meuse, eastward to the German border. Over 2 % of the people are coal-workers. *Iron* is also worked in the east, and deposits of *zinc* are mined near the Ardennes.

People.

The majority of the people are Roman Catholics, and number over seven millions. Belgium is, therefore, the most densely populated country in Europe, for the average density of population is over 650 to every square mile. The large towns near the coalfields contain most of the people, and the pastoral Ardennes have the scantiest population.

Industries, Communications, and Commerce.

The abundance of coal has developed large industrial centres along the Scheldt and Meuse. Liège, Namur, Charleroi, and Mons are iron-working centres. Cottons and linens are made at Ghent. Lace is made at Brussels, and woollen goods at Liège and Verviers, near the Ardennes pastures, the wool from which is supplemented by imports from South America. There are in the country nearly 100 beet-sugar factories, producing about 250,000 tons of sugar annually.

The rivers have been deepened, and are much used. The Scheldt below Ghent is canalised, and is navigable for large vessels to the sea. Canals have been made between other rivers and the sea. The railways converge on Brussels.

The chief imports are wool, wheat, minerals, and rubber; and the chief exports woollen goods, rubber, wheat, flax, and machinery. Belgium imports goods from France and the United Kingdom; and exports goods chiefly to Germany, France, and the United Kingdom. The chief port of the country is *Antwerp*, near the mouth of the Scheldt. Antwerp does much trade with London. *Ostend*, the chief packet-station, has a daily service with Dover.

Administration and Towns.

Belgium is governed by a King, and two Houses of Parliament—the Chamber of Representatives and the Senate.

Brussels, the capital (population half a million people), has carpet and lace factories. *Antwerp*, the seaport, *Liège*, the centre of the iron trade, and *Ghent*, a textile centre, are next in size to Brussels.

Holland.

Position, Surface, and General Features.

Holland, or the Netherlands, lies north of Belgium, west of Germany, and south and east of the North Sea. It lies in latitudes similar to those of East Anglia, but between meridians 3° 30′ E. and 7° E. Holland is one-tenth the size of the British Isles.

Nearly all the country stands on the delta of the Rhine and of its tributary the Maas (Meuse of Belgium). As these slow-moving rivers reach the sea, their suspended matter is dropped, raising the levels of the beds of the rivers, and of their banks, and so tending to flood the surrounding district. The Dutch have strengthened these banks by building stone dykes on them to a height above that of the highest known floods. The low-lying land between two dykes is pumped dry after rains, etc., by wind-mills, which are to be seen everywhere. The fertile meadows so produced are known as *polders*. In a similar manner the sea has been driven westward and northward. More than one-third of the 'dry' land lies below sea-level, and more land is being reclaimed every year from the sea. In the low land of the south-west, the many rivers have cut the land up into numerous islands, the chief of which is Walcheren. Near the coast much of the land is covered by sand which has been blown eastward from the shallow shores, forming sand-dunes having in some places a height of 30 ft. The Frisian Islands to the north of the mainland are parts of the old coastline.

The altitude of the land increases as we go eastward, until near the Meuse in the south-east a height of over 1000 ft. is reached.

Climate and Natural Productions.

The average air-temperatures of Holland are a little lower than those of Belgium, but they are fairly equable. The mean annual rainfall is higher than that of East Anglia, being about 28 inches. Rye, potatoes, oats, and sugar-beet are the most important crops. Bulbs are extensively cultivated in the north-west for export. The polders are well suited for cattle-rearing, and from these low-lying districts there are large exports of dairy produce. In the north horses are bred. The North Sea fisheries are valuable, and oysters are obtained from the muddy coasts. Minerals are practically absent.

People, Communications, and Commerce.

There are nearly seven million people in the country, the majority of whom are Protestants.

The staple industries are those connected with agri-culture. Butter, margarine, cheese, leather, spirits, and sugar are the chief products, and one-third of the workers are engaged in these industries.

The flatness of the country has enabled the Dutch to connect all the towns by means of canals. The largest of these are the North Sea canal, running to Amsterdam; a large canal joining Amsterdam to the Rhine; and the Rotterdam Waterway, enabling ocean-going vessels to

reach that port. The position of the country at the
mouth of a great river has made the Dutch a commercial nation, and has developed the canal ports of
Rotterdam and *Amsterdam* into the. most important
towns in Holland. More than 60 % of the total trade of
the country passes through Rotterdam. The mainland
packet-station of the *Hook of Holland* has a daily service with Harwich, and the island station of *Flushing*
has connection with Queenborough and Folkestone.

Rotterdam

Both Germany and Belgium have excellent communication by water with the North Sea and Atlantic Ocean
via Holland. Consequently their exports and imports
form a large part (two-thirds) of the trade of Holland.
Considerable trade is also carried on with the British
Isles, the Dutch exports being margarine, cheese, and
sugar. From British markets the Dutch import cotton
goods, coal, iron, and machinery. Rice and coffee (grown
in the Dutch East Indies) are noteworthy imports and
exports of Holland.

Administration and Towns.

The Sovereign is assisted in the government of the country by an Upper, or First, Chamber, and a Second Chamber, which together are known as the States General and meet at The Hague. *Amsterdam*, the centre of a diamond-cutting industry, and *Rotterdam* (each with about half a million inhabitants) are both large ports. *The Hague* is the capital; *Utrecht* is an important railway junction; and *Groningen* is a market for agricultural produce.

Germany.

Position and Size.

The northern boundary of this country is almost entirely formed by the North and Baltic Seas. A small portion of Germany occupies the peninsula of Jutland, and is separated by a land boundary from Danish Jutland. West of Germany lie Holland, Belgium, and France. To the south are Switzerland, Austria and Czecho-Slovakia; while on the east there is Polish territory. E. Prussia on the shores of the Baltic and east of the Vistula is now separated from Germany by Polish territory and by the Free City of Danzig. The area of Germany is 1½ times that of the British Isles.

Surface and General Features.

The Jura Mts run from France north-east through Switzerland, and through Germany under the name of the Franconian and Swabian Jura. This direction is continued by the Ore Mts. The Lower Rhine Highlands, a continuation of the Ardennes, run in the same S.W.—N.E. direction. The Bohemian Forest and the Sudetes run N.W.—S.E. The Bavarian Plateau lies between the Jura, the Bohemian Forest and the Alps; and the Black Forest lies west of the Jura. Northern Germany is a vast plain.

The Rhine at Bingen

Divides, Rivers, and Lakes.

The Jura form an important divide, from the north of which rivers run northward to the Rhine. From the south of this divide runs the Danube, having at first a north-easterly course, and reaching its most northerly point at Ratisbon. Then the river runs south-east, and passes out of Germany between the Alps and the Bohemian Forest. From this point the divide runs again north-east, shedding northward the Elbe and the Oder. The Elbe, receiving many tributaries from the Czecho-Slovakian slopes of the Bohemian Forest, Sudetes, and Ore Mts, breaks through the last-named mountains in a very beautiful gap, after which it runs north-west through Germany. The Oder runs north-west on the eastern side of the Sudetes.

The Rhine, the longest watercourse in Germany, rises at high altitudes in the Swiss Alps. The height of these mountains causes such low air-temperatures that most of the water vapour in the atmosphere falls to earth as the solid, snow. During the winter months this snow accumulates in deep snowfields. In the summer months most of this snow melts, and the water produced helps to swell the Alpine tributaries of the Rhine at a time when other rivers are usually shrinking in size. The Rhine and its tributaries run north to Lake Constance. The river, after leaving this lake, runs in a westerly direction through the Jura Mts, forming the Falls of Schaffhausen among others, and also forming the natural boundary between Germany and Switzerland. At Basel the Rhine turns, and runs northward through a deep valley separating Germany from France for over 100 miles. The Lower Rhine Highlands turn the river westward for about 25 miles, until it breaks through these Highlands in a beautiful gorge (or gap) between Bingen and Coblenz. From Coblenz, the river takes a north-westerly course, until near the Dutch border it turns west to form its delta. It has two very large tributaries, the Main on the east bank, and the Moselle on the west bank.   Near the end of its German course, the Rhine receives from the east the Ruhr.

The largest German lakes are found in the Pregel basin in East Prussia. Along the Baltic coast the rivers empty into a series of lagoons, or haffs.

Coast.

The western coast, washed by the North Sea, is the more important coast to the Germans.   The ports along this coast are never frozen.   The Baltic coast is low and shallow, and is bordered by sand-dunes.   Owing to the freezing of the surface waters of the Baltic Sea in winter, the ports along its coast are usually closed by ice during the winter months.

Climate.

Air-temperatures in the south are not much higher than in the north, because of the increase in altitude as we go southward.   The extreme east of the lowlands is warmer in summer and colder in winter than are the western parts.   Rainfall decreases in amount in an easterly direction, there being a rainfall varying from 27 inches in the west to 20 inches in the east.   On the western slopes of the southern highlands the rainfall in places is over 40 inches each year.

Plants and Animals.

The lowland part of Germany is in the zone of deciduous forests, bearing chiefly oak and beech trees. In the higher land to the south coniferous trees thrive better ; and the Germans have, during the last few years, increased the area covered by coniferous (pine, fir, and spruce) trees by planting these trees in place of deciduous trees.   The chief wooded regions are the highlands of the Black Forest and the Bavarian Plateau.

Wild animals, such as the red deer, boar, and elk, are found in the forests, while the chamois is found in the highest parts of the German Alps.

Agriculture.

The greater part of the land surface of Germany is productive, and more than half of this is devoted to agriculture. The cool climate of north Germany causes rye and oats to be cultivated, and these are replaced

In the Black Forest

in the south-west by barley and wheat. Potatoes are a very important crop. The sugar-beet is extensively cultivated in the middle parts of the valleys of the Elbe and Oder. Hops are cultivated in the middle Rhine valley, and the vine in the valleys of .the Rhine and its tributaries. In the moist plains of the north-west and south-west large numbers of cattle and horses are reared. Flocks of sheep are kept in the dry north-east. Pigs are almost as numerous as cattle.

Fisheries.

Fresh-water fish, especially salmon, are abundant in all the German rivers, except the Danube. On the shallow, muddy sea-floor north-west of Germany oysters are cultivated, and over the Dogger Bank German boats fish for cod, etc.

Minerals.

Coal. 2 °/₀ of the working people are coal-workers. The chief coal district, known as the Westphalia and Rhenish Prussia coalfield, is in the lower Ruhr valley. On the north-west side of the Ore Mts, near the Elbe, lies the second coalfield of Saxony. Near the source of the Oder, and east of the Sudetes, occurs the Silesian coalfield; the inhabitants of this district are to decide by the vote whether their country shall become a part of Poland or remain German. *Iron* ore is mined south of the Ruhr coalfield (in the Sieg valley). Through the restoration of Lorraine to France, the annual output of iron-ore in Germany falls from 36 to 6 million tons (pre-war figures). *Silver, copper, lead,* and *zinc* ores are also mined, chiefly in the Ore Mts. In the middle Elbe basin there are deposits of *rock-salt,* and of other earthy minerals.

If Upper Silesia becomes Polish, Germany will lose over a third of her pre-war annual output of coal, three-fourths of her zinc-ore, and a half of her lead-ore.

People and Religion.

The Germans number 55 millions, and are most numerous.in the coal-districts and in the Rhine valley. There are nearly twice as many Protestants as there are Roman Catholics ; and about 1 °/₀ of the people are Jews. Germany has many universities, and a large number of technical and secondary schools.

Industries.

A third of the people are dependent on agriculture; and many of the industries (e.g. the spirits, sugar, and wine manufactures) are dependent on local supplies of agricultural products. Wine is made in the Rhine valley, and beer is brewed in the south-west plateau. The root crops (beet and potatoes) have developed large sugar factories and distilleries for the manufacture of spirits between the lower Elbe and Oder basins; the coniferous forests of the highlands have given rise to lumbering and wood-carving industries.

The metal and textile industries are all centred near the coalfields. Iron and steel manufactures are very important in the Ruhr district, especially at Essen. Pig-iron has to be imported in large quantities to support the trade of this district. In the double town of Elberfeld-Barmen there are large woollen and cotton factories, and there are woollen factories at Aachen. A silk industry is carried on at Crefeld. The Saxony coalfield has developed woollen industries at Chemnitz, where machinery is also made. Dresden and its neighbouring towns near this coalfield form the 'Potteries' of Germany. Ship-building is carried on at the mouth of the Elbe.

Communications.

The slow movement in the lower parts of the German rivers has made them very important as means of communication. The Rhine is navigable for ocean-going steamers up to Cologne, and is constantly being improved. The Elbe can be navigated by small vessels throughout its German course. Vessels of all nations, and their cargoes, now have the same rights and privileges as are granted to German vessels and cargoes throughout the German courses of this country's rivers and canals. Of these canals, the chief is the Kiel canal, which is 60 miles long. Another important canal system connects Berlin with the Elbe and with the Oder. Railways have been constructed in all directions from Berlin, no German town being more than 24 hours' journey from the capital.

Commerce and Ports.

Before the outbreak of war in 1914, Germany ranked second to the United Kingdom in the list of the commercial countries of the World. The value of the total annual trade exceeded £1,000,000,000. Germany's imports and exports were very similar in character to those of the United Kingdom. In 1913, Germany sent goods worth over £80,000,000 to Britain, receiving goods valued at half that amount. The chief goods imported into Britain were sugar (made from beetroot), cotton goods, and iron and steel goods. By the Treaty of Versailles, Germany has to supply free to France about 10,000,000 tons of coal from 1920 until 1930.

Hamburg is the greatest German port. Coal, iron, petroleum, and various food-stuffs form its chief imports. The neighbouring port of *Bremen*, with its outport of *Bremerhaven*, is also noteworthy. *Stettin, Rostock*, and *Königsberg* are large Baltic ports.

Free zones are now maintained in German ports, and goods entering or leaving these free zones are not subject to any import or export duty, unless the goods are taken into or out of Germany. A charge is levied on each vessel which uses one of these zones. In both Hamburg and Stettin, there are free zones for the use of the Czecho-Slovak State. *Danzig* is now a Free City, and is no longer a part of Germany.

Administration.

Germany is now a Republic, the abdication of the German Emperor being announced on 9th Nov. 1918. The President of the Republic is elected for seven years, and he is assisted in the government of Germany by a *reichstag* and a *reichsrat*.

Towns.

Berlin, the capital of Prussia and of Germany, is a railway centre. Many of its two million inhabitants are employed in the printing and chemical industries. *Hamburg*, the great German port, is next in size. *Munich*, in the Danube basin of Bavaria, is the capital of the kingdom of Bavaria. It has renowned art galleries and libraries, and it is said to be the greatest beer-brewing

Nuremberg

town in the world. *Dresden* has large iron and porcelain industries. *Leipzig*, on the R. Saale, is the centre of a large book trade. It has fairs three times every year. *Breslau*, on the Oder, has developed because of its west-east trade between Saxony and Russia. *Cologne*, on the Rhine, is a railway centre. *Frankfort*, on the Main, is a commercial town, having fairs similar to those of

Leipzig and Breslau. *Nuremberg*, in the Bavarian Plateau, is the centre of important wood industries.

Denmark.

Position, Surface, and General Features.

Denmark occupies the peninsula of Jutland and several islands near the mouth of the Baltic. It has one-eighth the area of the British Isles.

Jutland is bounded on the west by the North Sea, on the north by the Skager Rak, and on the east by the Kattegat. Its west coast is low, and is bordered by sand-dunes, providing no harbours. The coasts of the islands, the chief of which is Seeland, are more useful as harbours. There are several straits between these islands, but the deepest is the Sound, between Seeland and Sweden. Nowhere is there any land more than 600 ft. above sea-level. Iceland and the Faeroes, which lie north-west of Denmark, are under Danish rule.

Climate and Natural Productions.

The air-temperatures of Denmark are similar to those of Scotland. The summer winds, bringing cool air from the surrounding seas, help to modify the natural temperatures, but in winter, when the Baltic is frozen, winds from that direction are cold. The rain-fall is similar to that of the German lowlands.

80 % of the land is productive. Oats, barley, and rye are the chief cereals. The moist meadows support over two million cattle, and dairy-farming and poultry-farming are very important.

Fishing is the chief industry of the inhabitants of the Atlantic islands. Minerals are scarce in Denmark. Peat is generally used for fuel.

People, Industries, and Commerce.

The Danes belong to the Scandinavian branch of the Teutonic race, and number three millions. Nearly all profess the Lutheran religion.

Over one-third of the people are dependent on agricultural pursuits for a livelihood. There is a small glove-making industry. Denmark has a good railway service, good roads, and numerous small canals.

The chief exports are provisions and eggs, and the chief imports are coal, textiles and manufactured goods. To the British Isles the country sends eggs, butter and bacon. In return, the British Isles send to Denmark coal, cotton and iron goods. The chief port is *Copenhagen*, on the east coast of Seeland, commanding all traffic through the Sound.

Administration and Towns.

The country is governed by a King, and two Chambers, which meet at *Copenhagen*. This, the only large town in the country, has a population of over half a million people.

Scandinavia.

Position and Size.

The peninsula of Scandinavia is bounded by the Atlantic Ocean on the west, the Skager Rak and Kattegat on the south, the Baltic and north Russia on the east, and the Arctic Ocean on the north. It is nearly 2½ times the size of the British Isles.

Surface and General Features.

The greater part of the land is mountainous, and the highest part lies very near the west coast. The western slopes, therefore, of Norway are very steep, and the eastern slopes of Sweden are more gentle. The southeast part of the Swedish peninsula is a low plateau, and between the high western and the low south-eastern plateaux there is lowland, occupied by several lakes.

Divides, Rivers, and Lakes.

The chief divide runs S.W.—N.E. and is near the west coast. Consequently, most of the western rivers are short and exceedingly swift, forming many waterfalls, which are both beautiful and useful. The eastern rivers are longer and much slower. The chief river of Norway, the Glommen, runs south-east. The largest river of Sweden runs parallel to the Glommen, and its lower course is known as the Gota. This, and several smaller rivers, feed the Swedish lakes, Vener, Vetter, and Mälar. Lake Vener is drained to the Kattegat by the R. Gota; the other two lakes drain to the Baltic Sea.

Coasts.

The northern and western coasts of Norway are very broken and indented. Fjords run for miles inland, but their mountainous shores provide no sites for ports. Numerous islands, the chief of which are the Lofoten Islands, lie off the western coast, and protect the shallow waters between them and the coast from the storm waves of the Atlantic Ocean. The coast of Sweden is low and fringed by sandy islands.

Climate.

For some days on either side of midsummer day, the sun never sinks below the horizon in the far north of this peninsula; and for similar periods on either side of midwinter day, the sun does not rise above the horizon. The west and south winds, blowing from the Atlantic Ocean, give to Norway a mild and rainy climate; but Sweden, which lies in the lee of the mountains, has an extreme and dry climate. In the highlands snow falls all the year round, giving rise to large snow- and ice-fields, from which immense glaciers are pushed seawards.

Natural Productions.

The high elevation and low air-temperatures render much of the land useless. In Norway three-quarters of the land is unproductive, and in Sweden one-third is unproductive. One-fifth of the land of Norway is under timber, as is one-half of Sweden. The pine is the chief tree growing in Scandinavia. Very little land can be cultivated, but Sweden has three times as much cultivated land as Norway. Potatoes and the cereals, oats, rye, and barley, are the chief crops. In the southern lowlands of Sweden a million sheep, as many pigs, and twice as many cattle are reared.

Fisheries are very important to the Norwegians, who catch large quantities of cod and herring, especially in

A Lapp encampment in Norway

the shallows between the islands and the west coast. There are also whale fisheries in the Arctic Ocean.

Minerals are becoming more important. There is only a little *Coal*, in the south of Sweden. *Iron* ore is abundant between L. Mälar and the R. Dal, and within the Arctic Circle at Gellivare.

The People.

The Scandinavians are a branch of the Teutonic family. Their religion is Lutheran. In the tundra of the north, the larger number of the people are Lapps. There are over two million people in Norway, and over five million in Sweden.

Industries, Communications, and Commerce.

The chief industry in both countries is lumbering, and associated therewith industries such as sawing and planing timber, joinery and furniture manufacture, the making of wood-pulp and paper. In Sweden a large iron-smelting industry is springing up. The Norwegian towns are all coast towns, having large fish trade.

The only navigable river is the Gota, which leads to L. Vener. From this lake a canal has been cut across the divide to L. Vetter, and by means of another canal access is given to the Baltic, without passing through the Sound. Railways have been laid through the lake plain and along the Glommen valley.

The chief exports of each country are timber and metals; and the chief imports are food-stuffs, coal, and manufactured goods (chiefly clothing). The chief ports are *Göteborg, Christiania,* and *Stockholm. Bergen* is a west coast fish port, and *Malmö* is the packet-station, trading with Copenhagen. *Narvik* in Norway and *Lulea* on the Baltic export the iron-ore from Gellivare.

Administration and Towns.

The Kings in each country are assisted in the government by a parliament. *Christiania* is the capital of

Norway. It has 250,000 people, and has a large timber trade. *Bergen* is the chief fish port, and *Trondhjem* is the old capital and a tourist centre.

Stockholm, the capital of Sweden, is built at the mouth of L. Mälar. It is half as large again as Christiania, and has large iron and steel works. *Göteborg*, the Swedish port, has exports of timber and metal goods. *Norrköping*, lying east of L. Vetter, is the chief manufacturing centre of Sweden.

Finland.

Finland lies between parallels 60° N. and 70° N. On the west it is bounded by the gulf of Bothnia, and by Sweden and Norway; it stretches eastward to about meridian 30° E. It is as large as the British Isles, but more than one-tenth of its surface (mainly in the south) is occupied by lakes. From the lake-studded plain, the land rises northward to the Scandinavian plateau. The climate of Finland is more extreme than that of Scandinavia. In the far north there are barren tundra, supporting only reindeer. Central Finland is forested, and the pine and spruce forests cover more than half the country. The southern part of the country has been partly cleared of forests, and in places the swamps have been drained. It is here that the cultivated area (one-tenth of Finland) is to be found. Oats, rye and barley are the chief crops. The population numbers over three millions, and the majority of the people are Lutherans. Agriculture and dairy-farming are the chief occupations. Paper, timber, tar and pitch, and butter are the principal exports (mainly to Britain). Food-stuffs and manufactured goods (chiefly from Germany) are imported. *Helsingfors* is the largest town, and *Abo* is the Baltic port. Finland became a Republic in 1919.

Russia.

Position and Size.

The eastern part of Europe, from the shores of the Arctic Ocean southward to the shores of the Black Sea, forms the country of Russia, which is 15 times as large as the British Isles. From north to south, as well as from west to east, Russia measures over 2000 miles.

Surface and General Features.

A part of the eastern boundary of Russia is the Ural Mts, high in the north and south, but quite low in the centre. In the southern Crimea peninsula there is a continuation of the Asiatic mountains—the Caucasus. The greater part of Russia is a plain, rising gradually to the Valdai Plateau, a large swampy district, the highest point of which is a little over 1000 ft. above sea-level.

The chief divide has a S.W.—N.E. direction, and the northward-flowing rivers are somewhat shorter and swifter than the large rivers flowing southward. The low elevation of the divide and its great distance from the sea have made these rivers extremely slow. The longest Russian river, the Volga, runs eastward and southward into the Caspian Sea. West of the Volga runs the Don, which at one point comes within fifty miles of the Volga. West of the Don lies the much longer Dnieper. This river and the Dniester empty into the Black Sea. The Neva drains the largest Russian lake, Ladoga.

Climate.

Air-temperatures increase as we go southward. The summer cooling, and winter warming, influence of the sea air is only felt in the western parts of the country. Generally the air-temperatures become more extreme in a south-easterly direction. The amount of rainfall diminishes in an easterly direction. The hills of the

Crimea cause the southern part of the Crimea peninsula to have heavy rainfall. The northern rivers are all frozen for a third of the year, as are the lakes.

Natural Productions.

The cold northern regions are tundra. Southwards small birch, larch, and fir trees lead to huge coniferous forests These gradually lead, south of parallel 60° N., to the deciduous forest zone, the trees of which have

A winter scene in Russia

been extensively cleared. The agriculture carried on in this zone produces rye, flax, and hemp. South of about parallel 50° N. the trees give place to grass lands, which are very dry in the east. The west is covered by a dark soil called 'black earth,' which is very much like leaf-mould. The wetter parts of this belt produce maize, and the drier parts wheat; and the eastern parts leading on to the Caspian depression are pastoral lands, on which horses and cattle are reared. The district south of the Crimea hills, having a Mediterranean type of climate, is

6—2

noted for such fruits as olive and grape, and in the east for cotton.

The extreme north is inhabited by the polar bear, arctic fox, and reindeer. The forest lands shelter the weasel, fox, bear, wolf, and many other fur-bearing animals. Salmon are caught in the northern rivers, and sturgeon in the Caspian rivers.

The mineral wealth is increasing in importance. *Coal* is very abundant in the hilly district between the Sea of Azov and the Donetz, a west bank tributary of the Don ; in the centre of the country at Tula, and in the low, central Urals. *Iron* ore is worked on all these coal-fields. Precious metals (*gold, platinum, silver*) and other minerals are mined in the central Urals.

People, Industries, and Commerce.

The majority of the Russian people are Slavs belonging to the Orthodox Greek Church. The total population of Russia-in-Europe is over 125 millions.

The majority of the people live in the country districts, only about 10 % being grouped in towns. They are chiefly engaged in lumbering, agricultural, and pastoral industries. The development of the mineral wealth is making the district round Moscow a large cotton-manufacturing centre, which gets its raw cotton from south Russia and from Turkestan. Tula is a large iron and steel working centre.

The low character of the country has encouraged the Russians to connect the upper courses of rivers by canals. It has also led to the development of a great railway system, which centres at Moscow. Much trade is still carried on by means of fairs—Kharkov, commanding the southern trade, and Nijni Novgorod, commanding the trade of central Russia, have large fairs..

The chief exports of Russia are cereals. The chief imports are manufactured goods, and raw materials, such as cotton and tea. The greatest trade of Russia before the war was carried on with Germany, after which came that with the United Kingdom. Russia sends to our

Petrograd

islands cereals, timber, eggs, and flax, and receives from us machinery and coal. *Petrograd* is the chief timber and grain port. The Arctic port is *Archangel*. *Odessa* is a large grain port on the Black Sea.

Administration and Towns.

Russia has been a republic since the abdication of the Tsar in 1917. South-west Russia is governed by the independent republics of the Ukraine and White Russia.

Petrograd, with two million inhabitants, is connected by canal with the gulf of Finland. It is a handsome city and a great port. *Moscow*, the old capital, has large iron and cotton factories. *Odessa*, on the northern shores of the Black Sea, exports large amounts of grain. *Kieff* is the centre of the sugar-refining and leather industries. *Kharkov* is a rising manufacturing town near the Donetz coalfield.

Poland.

Position and Size.

Poland is bounded on the west by Germany, on the south by Czecho-Slovakia and Rumania, on the east by the Ukraine and Russia, and on the north by the Duna, Lithuania and E. Prussia. It reaches the southern shores of the Baltic for about fifty miles between the Free City of Danzig and Germany. Its area is more than half as large again as that of the British Isles.

General Features and Natural Productions.

Poland is a great plain occupying the basin of the Vistula, which rises in the Karpathians to the south. Posen is in the Oder basin. The climate is more extreme than that of Germany, and the winter rainfall is less than the summer rainfall. A quarter of the country is forested, and more than a half is cultivated, or used for pasture. Rye is the largest crop raised. *Coal* is worked about ten miles north of the point where the Vistula first crosses the fiftieth parallel. 90 % of the coal raised on this coalfield is obtained (near Königshütte) in Upper Silesia, but it is probable that this district will become a part of Poland. This 'plebiscite area' also produces three-fourths of the *zinc* ore and a half of the *lead* ore of Germany. *Salt* is mined near *Cracow*. 5 % of the total *petroleum* output of the world comes from between *Borislav* and *Stry* (50 miles S.S.W. of Lemberg).

People, Industries, and Commerce.

There are about 23 million people in Poland, the majority being Slavonic in race and Roman Catholic in religion. With the inclusion of the plebiscite areas, Poland will gain two million people.

The majority of the people are workers on small farms. About two millions are settled in the large towns. *Lodz* (population 500,000) is a very important centre for cotton and woollen industries.

There is likely to be a considerable export (mainly to Germany) of rye, oats, potatoes and beet-sugar, since by the restoration of Posen and W. Prussia to Poland, Germany has lost about a third of her sugar, meat and breadstuffs. Raw materials (wool, cotton and jute) and machinery are the chief imports.

Poland has the free use of the waterways and docks of the Free City of Danzig, as well as a 'free area' in that port.

Towns.

The capital *Warsaw* (population 800,000) is a great commercial city. *Lodz* is the textile centre. *Lwow* (Lemberg) is the railway and commercial centre of the Karpathian territories. *Posnan* is the largest town in Posen.

Czecho-Slovakia.

Position and Surface.

The Czecho-Slovak State comprises Bohemia, Moravia, Silesia, Slovakia and Ruthenia. It is about half the size of the British Isles. It is bounded on the north by Germany and Poland, and on the south by Rumania, Hungary and Austria.

The Bohemian Forest, Ore Mts, Giant Mts and Sudetes are the limits of the Bohemian plateau on the S.W., N.W., and N.E. respectively. This plateau is drained northward by the Elbe, the chief tributary of which is the Moldau. Moravia occupies the basin of the March, a tributary of the Danube. Silesia extends from the Sudetes to the upper Oder, and the boundary between Czecho-Slovakian Silesia and Polish Galicia runs approximately along the divide between the basins of the Oder and the Vistula. The Oder gap between the Sudetes and the Karpathians is known as the Moravian Gate. Slovakia and Ruthenia include the high, western Karpathians, and a small part of the Danube plain.

Climate and Natural Productions.

The climate of western Czecho-Slovakia is like that of S.W. Germany, but the climate of the Karpathian territories is more severe. Rain falls chiefly in summer and most abundantly in the Karpathians.

The mountain slopes are forested, chiefly with pines, oak and beech trees. There are valuable sheep pastures on the lower slopes. The soil is generally fertile; potatoes, beetroot, oats, rye, barley and wheat are the staple crops. Maize is cultivated in Slovakia, and hops on a large scale in Bohemia. Apples, pears and stone fruit are also important.

Coal is mined between Prague and Plzen, and coal and *iron* ore are mined in the Oder basin (Witkowitz). The rich mineral district of Slovakia, which produces *precious metals*, iron and lignite, lies between meridians 19° E. and 21° E. and near parallel 48° 45' N.

People, Industries, and Commerce.

There are 14 million people in the Czecho-Slovak Republic; the majority are Slavs, and most of them are Roman Catholics. A third of the population is occupied in agriculture, with which are associated large sugar, beer, and spirit industries. The manufacture of textiles, glass, furniture and gloves is important. The Slovakia mining district has large metal works at Schemnitz and Kremnitz.

Sugar, fruit and hops, timber and coal, and glass form the principal exports, and food-stuffs, cotton and raw wool the imports. Poland has outlets to the sea *via* the Elbe and the Danube, and it has 'free areas' at Hamburg and Stettin. *Bratislava* (Pressburg) is the port on the Danube.

Administration and Towns.

Czecho-Slovakia is a republic, and the government is in the hands of a President, a National Parliament and a Senate.

Prague, the largest town in Bohemia (600,000 in-habitants), has large textile and iron industries. *Brno* has many wool mills, and *Plzen* has glass works, breweries and sugar refineries. *Bratislava* is a very busy industrial centre.

Austria and Hungary.

Position and Surface.

The separate republics of Austria and Hungary lie in the middle of Europe. Austria is one-fourth, and Hungary one-half the size of the British Isles. Germany and Czecho-Slovakia lie to the north, Rumania to the east, Jugo-Slavia and Italy to the south, and Switzerland to the west of these two republics, neither of which has now any control of the Adriatic coast. The Alps occupy the greater part of Austria, but the northern part of Austria in the Danube valley has a low elevation. A low range of hills (about as high as the Pennines in England) runs through Hungary from S.W. to N.E. North-west Hungary is a plain surrounding the Danube. Hungary, east of the Danube, is a vast plain through which the Tisza runs from north to south. South-west Hungary is hilly but it sinks towards Lake Balaton which is as large as Middlesex. The Drave and its tributary the Mur form the southern boundary of Hungary.

Climate and Natural Productions.

Air-temperatures are high in summer and low in winter on the Hungarian plain. Alpine Austria has cool summers and cold winters, and snow lies perennially on the higher Alps. The rainfall is heavier in Upper and Lower Austria than in Hungary; the greater amount falls in summer.

Forests of deciduous trees and, in the higher parts, of coniferous trees cover a large part of Austria and N. Hungary. Rye, barley and oats are the chief crops in Austria, and these together with maize (in the south) and wheat (in the north) are the principal Hungarian crops. Vines are cultivated on the southern slopes of the Hungarian hills near Tokaj. Large numbers of horses and cattle are raised on the pastures of the Hungarian plain, pigs in the maize belt, and sheep on the mountain pastures. Practically all the mineral areas formerly in Austria and Hungary have passed into the control of Czecho-Slovakia, Rumania and Jugo-Slavia. A little iron-ore and lignite are worked N.W. of Graz.

People, Industries, and Communications.

Austria has over 6 million and Hungary more than 11 million inhabitants. Most of the people are Roman

Catholics. Agricultural and pastoral industries are the principal support of the people.

The valley of the Danube is of the greatest import- ance as a line of communication between western and south-east Europe. Below Linz the valley narrows and 50 miles from that town it turns northward through a deep gorge (the Austrian Gap or Gate), and thence eastward through a small plain. The forested hills behind Vienna then turn the Danube southward into

Vienna

a wider plain, and after running for 40 miles the river again breaks through the hills by the gap which has Bratislava in Czecho-Slovakia at its eastern end. The Danube now runs eastward for 100 miles through the west Hungarian plain until it reaches the Hungarian hills. The gap by which the river passes through these hills is the Hungarian Gate ; Budapest is at its southern end. The Danube is navigable for steamers between Ratisbon in Germany and the Black Sea. From Vienna railways run westward *via* the Austrian Gate to Bavaria and France, northward to Bohemia, Dresden and Berlin, north-east *via* the March and the Moravian Gate to Poland and Russia, eastward to the Hungarian Gate and thence to the Black Sea and the Bosporus, and south-west to Italy.

Administration and Towns.

Austria was proclaimed a republic on the 12th November, 1918, and Hungary became an independent republic four days later.

Vienna, the capital of Austria (population two millions) is an important railway centre, and it has clothing, leather and beer industries. *Graz* has large iron-works. *Budapest* (population 900,000) is the chief town of Hungary and the centre of the flour-milling industry. *Szeged* in southern Hungary has tobacco factories.

Rumania.

North of Jugo-Slavia and Bulgaria, east of Hungary and south of Czecho-Slovakia, Poland and the Ukraine lies the Kingdom of Rumania. It is bounded on the east by the Black Sea and it is as large as the British Isles.

A half of Rumania is occupied by the Karpathians, Transylvanian Alps and Transylvanian plateau. The eastern plains which are drained by the Pruth and Sereth to the Danube and by the Dniester are covered with the fertile 'black earth.' The southern plains which drain southward merge into swamps near to the Danube. The climate of the plains is extreme, being hot in summer and cold in winter; most of the rain falls in summer. There are much colder conditions in the mountainous districts, and greater precipitation. The mountain slopes are forested, pines and firs predominating at higher altitudes and beech, oak and other deciduous trees at lower levels. Agriculture is the mainstay of the people, maize and wheat being the chief crops.

Petroleum springs are important in the middle Sereth valley, *iron* ores in the upper Maros valley, and *coal* in the Banat in the south-west.

The people number 17 millions, and they are governed by a King, a Senate and a Chamber of Deputies. Communication by the Danube is carried on by small steamers, the shallows at the Iron Gate being avoided by a canal. Railways from Hungary and the Banat follow the Temes valley up stream, and passing through a saddle reach Orsova *via* a small N.—S. valley. The Orsova-Bukarest railway crosses the Danube at the Cernavoda bridge on its way to Kustenje, the Black Sea port. This is the only railway bridge across the Danube between Beograd and the Black Sea.

Bukarest, the capital, has over 300,000 inhabitants. *Chisanau* (Kishinev) and *Cernauti* (Czernowitz) are large towns in Bessarabia and Bukovina respectively. *Galatz* is the principal grain port.

The Balkan Peninsula.

Position and Surface.

South of Austria, Hungary and Rumania lies the Balkan Peninsula, containing six countries, the total area of which is nearly twice that of the British Isles. This peninsula is bounded by the Adriatic, Ionian, Mediterranean, and Ægean Seas, the long, narrow Dardanelles, the Sea of Marmora, the short, narrow Bosporus, and the Black Sea.

Jugo-Slavia, Montenegro and Albania occupy the north-western, and Bulgaria the north-eastern, portions of the peninsula. Turkey-in-Europe with an area about equal to that of county Durham lies immediately to the west of the Bosporus. The rest of the peninsula is Greek territory.

Near the west coast, the Dinaric Alps run southward into the Morea; and the north-east is occupied by the Balkan Range. Between the two ranges, a high and wide plateau rises to over 10,000 ft. Macedonia is cut off from Bulgaria by the Rhodope Mts. The Morava valley of Serbia leads by a low saddle to the southward-flowing river Vardar, which empties into the Gulf of Salonika. The eastward and southward-flowing Maritza forms a valuable route from Bulgaria to Thrace. Northern Jugo-Slavia is a lowland, drained by the Save.

Climate and Natural Productions.

The island of Crete has the highest air-temperatures in Europe. Southern Greece has an equable climate, while the broader and more mountainous lands to the north have an extreme climate, especially in the east. The rainfall is greatest in the west and more rain falls in winter than in summer. The peninsula's products are maize, wheat, and other cereals. The vine, olive, fig, lemon, and plum are grown in the lower parts, and silk, tobacco, and cotton are also produced. The Morea is noted for currants. Sheep are more important than cattle. Pigs and goats are also pastured. More than one-third of the land is covered with deciduous forests. *Coal, iron* ores and *copper* ores are worked in places. By the terms of the Treaty of Neuilly, Bulgaria has to supply free 50,000 tons annually of coal to Jugo-Slavia from the Bulgarian State Mines at Pernik.

People, Commerce, and Ports.

There are 27 million people in the Balkan Peninsula. The Serbs, Croats and Slovenes of Jugo-Slavia, and the Montenegrins and Bulgars speak the Slavonic tongue. The Greeks are a separate branch of the Aryan race. All these people are Christians. The Turks are Mohammedan Mongols.

The chief industry is agriculture. Pastoral industries are important in the hilly districts. Roads are bad, and the best routes are from the Morava valley, southward to the Vardar valley, or eastward up the Nishava and through the Dragoman pass to the Maritza valley. Railways follow each of these routes. In the N.W., the railway from Austria to Italy follows the valley of the Save. A canal across the isthmus of Corinth connects Athens with the western seas. The easiest communication is by sea, and trade is chiefly in the hands of Greek sailors. The chief exports are grain, wool, fruit,

A Montenegrin street-musician

and olive oil. Manufactured goods form the chief imports.

Austria, Hungary and the United Kingdom are the best customers of the Balkan States. The chief ports are *Varna, Constantinople, Salonika, Piraeus* and *Fiume*.

Administration and Towns.

Jugo-Slavia, Bulgaria, Greece and Montenegro have Kings and parliaments. Turkey is governed by a Sultan and a parliament. *Constantinople*, with a million in-

habitants, is the trading centre of the 'Near East.'
Athens, with one-sixth of this population, is the capital
of Greece. *Salonika* is second in importance to Constantinople as a port of this peninsula. *Adrianople* is a
large town on the railway from the Turkish capital up
the Maritza valley. *Beograd*, the capital of Serbia, on the
south bank of the Danube, trades by rail with Salonika
and Constantinople. *Piraeus* is the port of Athens; and
Sofia is the capital of Bulgaria. *Laibach* in the north-
west is on the route from Italy to eastern Europe.

Switzerland.

Position, Size, and Surface.

The area of Switzerland is one-eighth that of the
British Isles, and it is surrounded by Germany, Austria,
Italy, and France. Three-fourths of Switzerland is mountainous. The country is divisible into three zones, that
of the north-west being the Jura. In the south, the Alps
occupy three-fifths of the whole area of Switzerland ; and
between the Alps and the Jura lies the Swiss plateau,
having an average height of 1000 ft. The St Gothard
peak, near the middle of the southern border, is the
starting point of four great valleys. The valleys running
north are occupied by tributaries of the Rhine, draining
Lakes Neuchâtel, Lucerne, and Zurich. Running east,
then north to Lake Constance, and then west, is the
Rhine. To the west of St Gothard runs the Rhone,
which drains through Lake Geneva; while the Ticino
runs southward to Lake Maggiore in Italy.

Climate and Natural Productions.

The high altitude of the country modifies all the air-
temperatures, so that the average air-temperatures are
those of more northerly countries. The altitude also
causes this country to have a very heavy rainfall and
snowfall, the equivalent depth in rain varying from

The Rhone Glacier, Switzerland

60 inches to 90 inches in the west, but much less in the north and east. The colder temperatures allow snow to remain in the higher parts all the year round, and so snowfields have developed, from which glaciers protrude far down the valleys.

A third of the land is covered with snow, or has a rocky surface. A quarter is under natural grasses, which lie between the upper limit of the tree-zone and the lower limit of the snowfields. These high pastures, known as alps, support many cattle. In addition to cattle, some pigs, goats, sheep, and horses are pastured. A quarter of the land is covered by crops (chiefly wheat), gardens, and fruit trees, while the remainder is forest. There are vineyards on the southern slopes of the Jura. There is practically no mineral wealth. The swift rivers and their waterfalls, however, provide wonderful water-power, which is being largely used for the generation of electricity.

People, Communication, and Towns.

The population numbers nearly 4 millions. The north-western people are Protestants, and the south-eastern people are Roman Catholics. Three people speak German to every one speaking French.

A third of the people are agriculturists. Manufactures are increasing in importance, cottons and silks being the chief. Watch-making is important in the towns at the base of the Jura. Machinery and electrical manufactures are increasing, though raw materials for all these industries must be imported, in addition to food-stuffs. The greatest part of the trade of this country is done with Germany.

Communication is naturally difficult. Railway tunnels pierce the Jura, and there is a network of railways across the plateau. The St Gothard tunnel connects the Reuss valley with the Ticino, the twelve-mile long Simplon tunnel to the west connects the upper Rhone valley with a tributary of the Ticino, and the Loetchberg connects Bern with the Rhone valley and Simplon.

The Government is a republic, with a President and two Councils. *Zurich* has 200,000 inhabitants, mostly engaged in textile industries. It is a great railway centre, as also are *Basel* and *Geneva* (the centre of the watch-making industry). *Bern*, the capital, is half the size of Zurich.

Italy.

Position and Size.

The peninsula of Italy lies to the south of Switzerland and Austria. It has a N.W.—S.E. direction, being bounded on the south and east by the Mediterranean, Tyrrhenian, and Adriatic Seas. With its island portions, Sicily and Sardinia, it has an area equal to that of the British Isles.

Surface and General Features.

The Alps occupy the north and west of Italy. The most important part of Italy is the low Plain of Lombardy, across which the river Po runs eastward. This river receives tributaries from the north and west, fed by the Alpine snows, rains, and lakes Maggiore, Como and Garda, and tributaries from the south, draining the Apennines. The Apennines start near Genoa and run south-east in parallel chains, keeping nearer the Adriatic than the Tyrrhenian coast. From the divide formed by this range, short, swift rivers run eastward, and longer rivers such as the Arno and Tiber run westward. The Adige, which rises near the Italian-Austrian frontier, runs west and then south through the Alps, and eastward over the plain, reaching the Adriatic a little south of Venice.

To the south-west of the Apennines, near Naples, there is a region of active volcanoes, the largest cone of which is Vesuvius. A similar district lies in north-east Sicily, where the largest cone is Etna.

Climate and Natural Productions.

The Alpine territories and the Plain of Lombardy have an extreme climate. The southern slopes of the Apennines have an equable climate. Rainfall is very heavy west of the Apennines, but diminishes in the Plain of Lombardy. The heaviest rainfall is in winter.

The lower slopes of the Po tributary valleys are

Vesuvius in eruption

irrigated by a network of canals, and produce wheat, maize and rice. The extreme climate of the Plain of Lombardy prevents the cultivation of olives, but the vine, mulberry, and citrus fruits are largely grown; while these and olives are produced in other parts of the country. Cattle and swine are bred in the northern plains, sheep and goats in the hilly districts. Tunny and mackerel fisheries are important in the western deep seas, whence sponges are also obtained. There is little mineral wealth. Sulphur is obtained from the volcanic cones, and marble from Carrara.

People, Communications, and Commerce.

There are 38 million people in Italy. The majority of them are Roman Catholics. A third of the people are agriculturists. Many of the industries, e.g. silk, wine, olive-oil, are dependent on agriculture. The silk industry is most extensively carried on in the Plain of Lombardy and in the Adige valley.

Within the last century, roadways have been made over the Alps to France, Switzerland, and Austria. But these are now supplanted by railways, which are carried by long tunnels through the mountains. The Mt Cenis tunnel in the west, Simplon and St Gothard in the centre (north of Lakes Maggiore and Como) and the Brenner in the east (to the north of Lake Garda) carry railways from France, Switzerland, Germany, and Austria. These railways run through the plains on the east side of the Apennines to Brindisi, while other routes lead from the Plain of Lombardy over the Apennines to Genoa and along the west coast. From Trieste an important route leads eastward to Laibach in the Save valley. There are numerous good ports round the coast, the chief being *Genoa, Naples, Leghorn, Palermo, Brindisi, Venice,* and *Trieste.*

The chief imports are wheat, raw cotton, coal and coke, machinery, iron goods, and fish. The chief exports are raw silk and silk goods, cotton goods, fruits, olive-oil, and wines. Much hemp and fresh fruit come to the British Isles from Italy.

Administration and Towns.

The King is assisted in the government of the country by a Senate and a 'Chamber of Deputies.' The largest town, with nearly three-quarters of a million inhabitants, is *Naples.* In the northern plain, *Milan* and *Turin* have silk, wine, and oil industries. *Rome*, the capital (with half a million people), contains the cathedral of St Peter, the largest church in Europe, and the Vatican, the residence of the Pope. *Palermo* is the Sicilian port, and *Genoa* the Mediterranean port of the northern plain. *Florence*, on the Arno, and its port *Leghorn*, are manufacturing centres. *Bologna* is a large commercial town, south of the Po valley. *Venice* and *Trieste* are the Adriatic ports of the north, and *Messina* is the eastern port of Sicily.

The Iberian Peninsula.

Position, Size, and Surface.

The south-west peninsular portion of Europe has a land boundary, France, on one-eighth of its margin only. The sea-shores form the other seven-eighths, and these shores are washed by the Bay of Biscay, the Atlantic Ocean, and the Mediterranean Sea. Spain is $5\frac{1}{2}$ times the size of Portugal, and together they are nearly twice as large as the British Isles.

The greater part of the peninsula is a high plateau, above which rise various parallel ridges. The plateau slopes generally westward. Its northern limit is formed by the Cantabrian and Iberian Mts, and its southern boundary is the Sierra Morena. North of the plateau, but quite independent of it, run the Pyrenees; while to the south-east the lofty Sierra Nevada form another range of mountains.

The Aragon lowland, which is drained by the Ebro, lies between the Pyrenees and the Iberian plateau. The lowland between the plateau and the Sierra Nevada is known as Andalusia, and is drained by the largest of the Iberian rivers, the Guadalquivir. From the plateau, the Tagus, Douro and other rivers flow westward, providing routes into the interior.

Climate and Natural Productions.

Air-temperatures increase generally in a southward direction, but the high altitudes of the interior cause a great lowering of these temperatures. The prevailing southward direction of the winds in summer gives to the north lower air-temperatures and heavy rains. In winter the prevailing winds are westerly, and the west gets the heavier rainfall and has milder air-temperatures.

An orange-grove in Spain

In the east coastal lowlands irrigation must be practised in order to cultivate the soils. The chief districts so cultivated are in the valley around Murcia, and in the valley around Valencia. The products of these irrigated districts are oranges and grapes. The coastal lowlands south of the Sierra Nevada produce sugar-cane, and Andalusia is a cattle- and horse-rearing district. The plateau is generally a sheep-grazing district, but in the wetter north, around the upper Douro, wheat is cultivated. The Aragon lowland, irrigated from the Ebro, is a wine-producing region. Portugal has generally a 'Mediterranean' climate, and produces the vine and fruits, wheat and maize. The greater part of the Spanish forests has been destroyed, but the forests in the west of Andalusia and south Portugal are noted for their cork bark.

Minerals are abundant in the Iberian Plateau, being chiefly mined in its northern and southern edges. From the Cantabrian Mts valuable *iron* ore is mined between meridians 6° W. and 2° W. *Coal* is mined in the west of this iron-field. To the south of it, and in Valencia, *lead* is mined. In the southern edge of the plateau, one-quarter of the world's output of *copper* is raised near *Huelva* and in the valley of the *Rio Tinto*, a few miles from the south-west border of Spain.

People, Communications, and Commerce.

The people of Spain are four times as numerous as those of Portugal, the total population being over 25 millions. The majority are Roman Catholics. Most of the people are agriculturists, or are supported by industries connected with locally produced agricultural products. Wine-making and the silk trade are the chief industries. Port is produced in the Douro valley, and collected at Oporto, while sherry is exported from Cadiz. At Barcelona there are cotton factories.

Communication everywhere is bad. Railways enter the country at each end of the Pyrenees, and connect with Madrid and the west coast ports. A railway also runs from north to south in the Portuguese coastal lowland. The rivers are navigable for small vessels only.

The chief exports are wine, ores, and fruits; and the chief imports are textiles, iron goods, machinery, and fish. The ports are *Bilbao, Oporto, Lisbon, Cadiz, Malaga*, and *Barcelona*.

Oporto

Administration and Towns.

Spain is a constitutional monarchy, the King being assisted in the government by a senate and congress. Portugal since 1910 has been a republic, with a President, and Lower and Upper Chambers.

Madrid, the capital and central town of Spain, has 650,000 people. *Barcelona* is a manufacturing centre *Lisbon* is the capital and the chief port of Portugal, and has over 400,000 inhabitants. *Valencia* is noted for raisins and oranges. *Oporto*, the second town of Portugal, exports wines. *Seville* and *Malaga* are fruit-growing centres.

CHAPTER V

ASIA

Position and Size.

The continent of Asia is the eastward continuation of Europe. The Ural Mts, Ural and Manich rivers form the chief boundaries on land between Asia and Europe, while the boundary between Asia and Africa in the west is a line drawn from the head of the Gulf of Akaba in a north-westerly direction to the Mediterranean Sea. In the west the Caspian, Black, and Mediterranean Seas, in the south the Indian Ocean, in the east the Pacific Ocean, and in the north the Arctic Ocean form the water boundaries. The land area is over one-third of that of all the land surface of the World.

Surface and General Features.

Asia is a continent of large plateaux, bounded by high ridges of mountains. A section across such a plateau resembles a section across an overturned saucer. The narrowest and highest of these plateaux is the Pamir plateau, from which three plateaux run west, east, and north-east. The western plateau passes from the Pamirs through Afghanistan to Persia, forming the wide Iran plateau, which is continued westward as the Armenian, and further west as the Anatolian plateau. The Anatolian plateau slopes gradually west to the Mediterranean Sea. Parallel to the northern edge of this plateau runs a great ridge of mountains—the Caucasus. A high saddle and two valleys occupy the land between the Caucasus Mts and the Armenian plateau.

The eastern plateau widens very rapidly from the Pamirs, to form the Tibet plateau, which sinks gradually eastward into the South China highlands. The northern boundary of the Tibet plateau is the Kuen Lun Mts, while in the south the Himalayas form a high barrier, with very steep southern slopes.

The north-east Tarim-Mongolian plateau is lower than either of the others, and bounded on the north-west by broad mountain chains, the Tian Shan, the Altai, and Yablonoi ranges. The plateau is shut in on the east by the Kingan Mts, and on the south by the high edge of the Tibet plateau.

The five large peninsulas of Asia are all mountainous. The Indo-China peninsula is a continuation of the Tibet plateau. The Indian peninsula consists of the Dekkan plateau, and Arabia is also a plateau. The two latter plateaux are not bounded by mountainous ranges. They are both highest in the west, and have steep slopes facing their western sea-coasts. Each plateau slopes very gradually eastward to the sea.

The remaining portions of Asia are valleys and plains. The chief of these are the Turan-Siberian plain, Mesopotamia valley, the Indus-Ganges valley, and the South and North China and Manchuria lowlands.

Divides, Rivers, and Lakes.

The chief divide runs north-east from the Pamir plateau. From the Tian Shan Mts run the Amu Daria and Syr Daria to the salt Aral Sea. Further north, the Obi, Yenisei, Lena, and other very large rivers drain to the Arctic Ocean. Between the Altai and Yablonoi Mts there lies the large fresh-water Lake Baikal, which is drained by the Angara, a tributary of the Yenisei. From the southern side of the divide the great Amur, rising in the Mongolian plateau, cuts its way through deep gorges to the Pacific. Near the Pamirs a group of rivers runs from this divide and from the northern slopes of the Kuen Lun Mts, joining to form the Tarim river, which empties into the marshy and salt Lob Nor.

From the Tibet plateau the large Chinese rivers, the Hoang-ho, Yang-tse-kiang, and Si-kiang, run eastward. The Song-ko, Mekong, Menam, Salwen, and Irawadi run southward ; and the Brahmaputra, on the north side of the Himalayas, runs for a long distance east, and suddenly turns south-east across the plateau's rim in deep and inaccessible gorges, finally turning west

The Yang-tse gorges

to the Ganges lowland. From the southern edges of the Pamir and Tibet plateaux the Indus and Ganges run to the Indian Ocean; and from the south edge of the Armenian plateau, the Euphrates and Tigris flow south-east through a common mouth to the shallow Persian Gulf. The Iran, Armenian, and Anatolian plateaux all contain salt lakes. To the north-west of the Arabian plateau, in a deep trough or rift, lies the Dead Sea, more than 1000 ft. below sea-level. This lake, fed by the swiftly flowing R. Jordan, is the saltest lake in the world.

Coasts.

The north coast is flat and is ice-bound for a great part of the year. The east coast is separated by Bering Strait from North America, and has five great bays occupied by the Bering, Okhotsk, Japan, Yellow, and the South China Seas. These seas are enclosed on the east by the Aleutian, Kurile, Japanese, Riu-kiu, and Philippine-Malay archipelagoes. The northern seas are also partly enclosed by the Kamchatka and Korea peninsulas and Sakhalin Island.

The Philippine-Malay archipelago includes some very large islands, all more or less mountainous. The largest of these islands are Luzon, Mindanao, Celebes, Borneo, Java and Sumatra. The Sunda Strait separates Java from Sumatra, and the latter island is separated from the Malay peninsula by Malacca Strait. The greater number of these islands, together with the above-named bow-shaped archipelagoes, have volcanic cones from which occasionally eruptions take place, accompanied by earthquakes.

The south coast has four large openings, the Bay of Bengal, Arabian Sea, Persian Gulf, and Red Sea. The Ganges-Brahmaputra, emptying into the Bay of Bengal, has formed a large delta of fine sediment. Similarly, the slow rivers draining the Dekkan plateau have formed deltas where they enter the Bay of Bengal. South of the Indian peninsula lies the mountainous island of Ceylon. The Dekkan, Iran, and Arabian plateaux, jutting out to the sea, have formed the rocky coasts of the Arabian and Red Seas. These coasts are, however, broken by the delta of the Indus and by the Persian Gulf. From the Arabian Sea the Gulf of Aden leads west to the very narrow Strait of Bab-el-Mandeb. This strait widens in a north-westerly direction to the deep Red Sea, which terminates in the north-east in the Gulf of Akaba. The Asiatic shores of the Mediterranean are rocky, providing few good harbours except in the extreme west.

Climate.

(a) Air-temperatures.

Very low air-temperatures are recorded in north-east Asia during the winter months. The air over the high plateaux is also very cold. Air-temperatures are highest in the south-east, the southern peninsulas having on the average air-temperatures like those of our hottest summers. In summer time the hottest air lies over the land to the west of India. Air-temperatures fall gradually from Turan to northern Siberia. Over the plateaux the air is much colder than over the lowlands in the same latitudes. There is a great range in temperature, from summer to winter, at places situated a long way from the seas, but less range near the coasts.

(b) Rainfall.

In winter, rains fall over the Mediterranean lands, Ceylon, and the Malay archipelago. The chief rains fall in summer, owing to the winds which then blow inland. South-eastern Asia receives very heavy falls of rain from these winds. On the lee side of the lofty rims of the plateaux little or no rain falls; and the plains of Turan and Siberia, which lie in the lee of the plateaux, are also very dry.

All the year round southern Asia should be under the influence of the north-east trade winds. But, as stated above, the summer winds blow inland; and in winter, the winds have the same direction as the trade winds. These periodic winds are known as *monsoons*.

Plants and Animals.

The northern lands are tundra, producing only mosses and small shrubs, and are the homes of reindeer and

arctic fox. The lowlands of Siberia are in the coniferous
and deciduous tree-belts. In the forests bears, foxes,
sables, and other fur-bearing animals are still abundant.
With increase of temperature, combined with less rainfall, the woods give place in the Turan lowland to
steppes with rich wheat lands in the north, pasture
lands in the centre, and desert land in the drier, warmer
southern parts.

The coastal countries in the south-east of Asia have
entirely different plant and animal life. With great

Tibetan and yak

heat and generally heavy summer rainfall, plants grow
abundantly. The coastal lands lying north of parallel
40° N. have products similar to those of Europe lying
in the same latitude. The lowlands south of this parallel
produce (in order going south) millet, maize, rice, and
other cereals; flax, hemp, cotton, and jute among the
fibres; and on the well-watered hill-slopes mulberry,
tea, coffee, and cacao. The tropical countries also pro-

duce sugar, indigo, and rubber, and important palms, such as bamboo and coco-nut. The wet, western slopes in the Tropics are densely wooded, and produce teak and other valuable hardwoods.

Everywhere elevation produces an alteration in the character of the plant life, so that, e.g., in the upper Brahmaputra valley in Tibet, barley and wheat are the summer crops, while in the corresponding lowlands of the Yang-tse-kiang rice is the typical cereal. In the upper Yang-tse-kiang and Indus valleys wheat is an important winter crop. Mediterranean types of fruits, etc. are produced where the land is irrigated in the western plateaux, and form a staple export of Turkey-in-Asia, Persia, and Arabia.

The animals of the monsoon lands include, in the hotter parts, tiger, leopard, elephant, rhinoceros, crocodile, and in the dense, tropical jungles, snakes. The cooler and drier plateaux provide pasture for sheep and goats. Camels are used in the desert areas as beasts of burden, horses on the wetter plains, elephants in the monsoon lands, and the yak (a species of ox) on the cold Tibet plateau. Fresh-water fish are abundant in the Siberian rivers, and there are some fisheries in the cold waters of the north-eastern seas.

Minerals.

The precious metals, *gold* and *silver*, are abundant in the mountainous districts round Lake Baikal. Gold is mined in the south of the Dekkan plateau, and *precious stones* are washed out of the river-gravels, especially in Ceylon and Burma. *Tin* ore is important in the Malay peninsula. *Iron* and *copper* ores outcrop in various parts of China and Japan. *Oil* is pumped from wells in the Indo-China peninsula, in the Tian Shan Mts, in the valleys of tributaries of the Syr Daria, and around the Caspian Sea. *Coal* outcrops in Japan, China, Borneo, and India.

Siberia, Caucasia, and Turkestan.

Position and Size.

The north and north-west parts of Asia comprise Siberia, Caucasia, and Turkestan. Bounded on the east and north by the Pacific and Arctic Oceans, the country narrows in a south-westerly direction, to include the Aral and Caspian Seas; and it is separated from Europe by the Ural Mts and river, and by the Manich valley, running from near the Caspian Sea north-west to the Sea of Azov. This great region lies north and north-west of the great Asiatic plateaux and is over 50 times the size of the British Isles, and forms a third of Asia.

Surface and General Features.

From meridian 80° E. a wedge of mountains runs north-east to East Cape, with its southern slopes drained by the Amur. The country lying north and north-west of this mountain belt slopes gradually to the Arctic Ocean, and is drained by many rivers, the chief being the Yenisei, with the Angara draining the large fresh-water Lake Baikal, and the Obi with the Irtish and Tobol.

The south-western plains lead southward to Turan, which is occupied by salt lakes. Many of its rivers lose themselves in the sands; but the great Amu Daria and Syr Daria empty into the salt Aral Sea. Caucasia consists of the slopes of the Caucasus Mts.

Climate.

The air-temperatures of Siberia, gradually increasing in a southerly direction, increase less rapidly in the mountainous east. Turan and Caucasia have the highest temperatures. Generally, all places have an extreme climate, with increasing severity as we go north. The amount of rainfall diminishes in a westward direction.

Turan has very little rain. Its rivers tend to dry up in summer. Caucasia receives more rain, and Trans-Caucasia has a Mediterranean type of climate.

Plants and Animals.

From the northern tundra little is obtained. Coming south and east, we find increasing growths of trees, until the Siberian taiga (or forest) of conifers is reached. This taiga also clothes the slopes of the plateau edges,

The Caucasus Mountains

and shelters many fur-bearing animals (bear, fox, marten, and sable). As the coniferous zone gives place southward to the deciduous zone, so this zone in turn gives place in the drier, warmer plains south of parallel 50° N. to grass lands with rich soil. These lands are being rapidly developed by Russian peasants and produce large amounts of wheat. Further south the vegetation becomes poorer, and is only fit for the rearing of horses, sheep, camels, and cattle by the nomadic Kirghiz tribes.

The rivers of Turan, creating oases both naturally and by irrigation, enable cotton, corn, tobacco, and various fruits to be grown. This is notably the case in the upper valleys of the Syr and Amu Darias and their tributaries. Caucasia in the north is pastoral, while south of the Caucasus Mts the climate is so genial that olives ripen, and cotton may be grown.

Minerals.

Caucasia and those parts of Turan lying on the north-east shore of the Caspian Sea are rich in *petroleum*. The district of Baku, south of the Asperon peninsula, has a valuable oil trade. In the Ferghana (upper Syr) district oil is also pumped. Caucasia has a *coal*field south-west of the Caucasus Mts. A large coalfield lies south of Tomsk and Krasnoyarsk. The mountainous parts of Siberia contain large deposits of *gold*, and this precious metal also occurs in the upper Amur basin. *Silver* and *iron* ores are also found.

The People.

Five out of every six people in Siberia are Slavs. One in three in Caucasia and one in eleven in Central Asia are Slavs. These represent invaders in the last few centuries. Of the remainder occupying Siberia, the majority are Tatars and Mongols; in Caucasia, there are more Mongols than in Siberia, while in Central Asia, six out of seven are Mongols. There are 13 million people in Caucasia, nearly 11 millions in Central Asia, and 10 millions in Siberia; and the numbers of people to every square mile are 74, 8, and 2 respectively.

Industries, Communications, and Commerce.

In Caucasia there are large oil-refineries, and silk and wine industries. Turkestan has leather and carpet industries. In Siberia there are several large mining centres, the chief being Irkutsk.

Along the Siberian railway Siberian timber, hides, and butter, together with Chinese and Japanese goods, are carried westward. The Central Asian railway collects wool, hides, cotton, and tobacco from Turkestan, and from Krasnovodsk goods are carried over the Caspian Sea to Baku, on its western shore. Large amounts of cotton are now taken to Moscow and other Russian cotton-working centres by the Trans-Caspian railway. This railway also does much trade in carrying petroleum from *Baku* to the Black Sea port of *Batum*, from which port the oil is carried in tank steamers to European markets.

Administration and Towns.

The whole of this region is split up into governments and provinces. Caucasia is split up into five independent republics. Turkestan and Siberia are under Bolshevik rule.

In **Caucasia** the chief town is *Tiflis*, with 300,000 inhabitants. It has silk, wool, and wine industries. *Baku* is the oil centre.

In **Turkestan** the capital *Tashkent*, served by the Central Asian railway, has a large trade in silk, cotton, etc. *Kokand*, south-east of the capital, has similar trade. *Merv, Khiva*, and *Samarkand* are situated in fertile oases.

In **Siberia**, *Irkutsk* is the oldest and largest town, and *Tomsk* the University town. *Vladivostok* is the fortified Pacific port.

The Empire of Japan.

Position, Size, and Surface.

The Empire of Japan stretches from parallel 50° N. to the Tropic of Cancer, and is insular and peninsular in character. It includes the southern half of Sakhalin Island, the Kurile Is., Hokkaido, Honshiu, Shikoku, Kiushiu, Riu-kiu Is., and in the south Formosa, together with the peninsula of Korea. The total area of this

Empire is twice that of the British Isles, the mainland of Honshiu being nearly as large as Great Britain.

The whole surface is occupied by mountains and by volcanic cones, from some of which eruption has taken place during the last century. The highest peak, Fuji-yama, is snow-capped for the greater part of the year. Earthquakes are very frequent. Rivers are everywhere short and swift, and very dangerous during the rainy season. There is a long, much indented coastline, which on the south and east of the mainland provides good harbours. The Sea of Japan is very rough during the winter months, and is liable to freeze; while the more northerly Sea of Okhotsk freezes every winter.

Climate and Natural Productions.

Air-temperatures increase in a southward direction, but the great variation in elevation counteracts the influence of the Sun's heat very much. The northern part of the Empire has an extreme climate, while in Taiwan air-temperatures are always high. The summer monsoon (south and south-east winds) brings abundant rain to the windward slopes. In winter cold winds blowing out from the Asiatic continent cause the western parts of the islands to have low temperatures, and cause rain and snow falls on the windward (in this case west-ward) slopes. At the change of monsoons, very small area low-pressure systems known as typhoons do great damage to shipping, as the force of the winds produced by them is great.

Forests cover nearly one-third of the land, the chief trees being the lacquer tree, camphor laurel, mulberry, sago-palm and various conifers. Tea-plantations cover the south-facing slopes of southern Honshiu, and the bamboo grows freely. Less than one-twelfth of the land is cultivated, producing wheat, millet, rice, soya-beans, tobacco, cotton, and indigo. Cattle, horses, and swine are reared. Fish, especially cod, are very abundant in the seas, and salmon and trout abound in the swift-flowing rivers.

The chief mineral of Japan is *coal*, which is mined in the west of Kiushiu, in Hokkaido, Korea, and Sakhalin. *Iron* ores are abundant. *Sulphur, copper, silver, gold,* and *petroleum* are also worked.

People, Industries, and Communications.

The Japanese are industrious and skilful. Their religions are Buddhism and Shintoism. Most of the people of Korea are Confucians. Education generally

A tea plantation in Japan

is in an advanced state. The population numbers 78 millions, being very dense in central and western Honshiu.

For centuries small industries have been carried on, but the recent rapid advance of the Japanese has brought to the country industries developed on European lines. Local supplies of coal and iron, cotton and silk, together with cheap food and clothing, have so developed the cotton and silk manufactures that recently over £70,000,000 worth of silk, and half that value of cotton piece goods, were made in one year; and over three-fourths of a million women were employed in these industries alone. There are large ship-building and iron and steel works in Kiushiu.

Communication is almost impossible along the rivers especially during the rainy season, but trade by sea between lowland and lowland has long been carried on. Roads are everywhere bad. There are now nearly 8000 miles of railway running through the Empire. Trade is carried on from the mainland to Korea through Fusan, the terminus of the railway which does part of the trade of Manchuria and China.

Commerce and Ports.

Imports and exports are almost of equal value, and together reach a total of over £400,000,000. Raw cotton is the largest import, forming nearly one-third of the total imports. Of the exports, raw silk is valued at more than one-fourth of the total, other exports being cotton yarn, silk goods, coal, matches, and copper. The greater part of the import and export trade is carried on with the United States of America, China, and British India. The chief ports are *Nagasaki*, *Yokohama*, and *Kobe*.

Administration and Towns.

Since 1889 Japan has had a constitutional government. The Emperor exercises the whole of the executive power, being advised and assisted by ministers, and houses of peers and representatives.

Tokyo, the capital, has two million inhabitants. It is a city of learning and of manufactures. Its port, 17 miles south, on the Bay of Tokyo, is *Yokohama*. *Osaka*, more than half the size of Tokyo, has ship-building and cotton industries. *Nagoya* is near large potteries, and *Kobe* is the port of Osaka. *Nagasaki*, on Kiushiu, is a rising

Korea: a street in the native quarter

port and coaling station. *Seoul* is the chief town of Korea. *Tainan* is the chief town of Formosa, from which island tea and camphor are exported.

China.

Position, Size, and Surface.

China lies in latitudes similar to those of the Mediterranean Sea and North Africa and occupies an area over 30 times that of the British Isles. It includes China and the following dependencies : Manchuria, Mongolia, Chinese Turkestan, and Tibet.

The greater part of the empire is made up of the low Tarim-Mongolia plateau and the high Tibet plateau.

From the latter three great rivers, the Hoang-ho, Yang-tse-kiang and Si-kiang run eastward. The lower Hoang-ho forms a great lowland, which opens out to the shallow Gulf of Chili. The mountainous Shantung peninsula forms the southern edge of this gulf. The lower part of the North China lowland is covered by wind-drifted yellow soil known as *loess*. This soil is very porous, and is rapidly cut into by streams, but it is extremely fertile when carefully irrigated. Draining into the north end of the Gulf of Chili is the small Liao river, the valley of which is bordered on the east by the Liao-tung peninsula, and by various mountain ranges. This lowland, together with the valley of a tributary of the Amur, forms Manchuria. Separated from the plain of China by the Pe-ling range, the Yang-tse-kiang runs from the Tibet plateau eastward to the Yellow Sea. It receives many important rivers, the chief being the Min and Han from the north. South of the Yang-tse-kiang, the South China highlands, 5° in width from north to south, shed rivers north to the Yang-tse-kiang and south to the Si-kiang, the most important waterway in south China.

Climate and Natural Productions.

The average air-temperatures of China decrease in a northward and westward direction. The monsoons are well marked. In summer the winds blow from the south, and in winter from northern quarters. The summer winds bring large quantities of rain, the fall of which decreases northward and westward. Mongolia, Turkestan, and Tibet have little rainfall, and the first two are deserts. Winter conditions are everywhere extreme, especially in the higher plateaux.

Agriculture is the mainstay of the people. Wheat, millet, maize, and rice are the most important cereals cultivated, rice being cultivated from the Yang-tse-kiang valley southward. The hill-slopes are everywhere terraced, and tea and mulberry plantations are very important. Tea is grown in the highland provinces between the Yang-tse-kiang and the Si-kiang and as far as Szechuan, the province drained by the Min. Silk-culture is, however, more important than tea, and is extensively carried on in Szechuan. Cotton is grown in the middle and lower Yang-tse-kiang valleys, and sugar is also produced here and in the south.

In some of the mountainous tracts the elephant, rhinoceros, tiger, bear, wolf, and other wild animals exist. The more settled parts of the dry interior pasture sheep and goats. The fisheries are everywhere important.

China is probably the richest *coal*-bearing country in the world. In the province of Shansi, bordered on the west and south by the Hoang-ho, anthracite coal-seams averaging 20 ft. in thickness crop out and dip at very low angles to the horizontal. They are estimated to underlie an area of at least 10,000 square miles. Large coalfields, as yet undeveloped, occur in Szechuan, and in the South China highlands. *Iron* ores are being worked in the Shansi coalfield, *copper* in the mountainous divide between the Si-kiang and Yang-tse-kiang, and *tin* south of the source of the Si-kiang.

The People.

Tribes in a high state of civilisation are said to have invaded China proper from the oases of Chinese Turkestan 4000 or more years ago. Spreading eastward to the lowlands they conquered the native races, teaching them various methods of irrigation learned in the plateau oases. A later invasion of pastoral races from Mongolia led to the construction of the Great Wall of China, west-ward roughly along parallel 40° N., in order to keep out these marauders. Three centuries ago the North China lowlands were again invaded,—this time by the Man-chus, who founded the dynasty which came to an end in February, 1911. China is now a republic.

A large number of the people are Confucians. Buddhists, in Tibet and Mongolia, and Mohammedans are also numerous. Recently great advance has been made in providing means of education, and universities, medical schools, technical institutes, etc. are being founded throughout the country. It is estimated that the people number 325 millions, a population three-fourths of that of the whole of the British Empire.

Industries, Communications, and Commerce.

Porcelain, paper-making, and the cultivation and weaving of silk have long been characteristic industries. Quite recently cotton, wool, and silk mills have

The end of the Great Wall on the Manchurian frontier of China

been erected at Shanghai, Canton, and Chifu. Flour and rice mills are becoming more numerous. The occurrence of local supplies of iron-ore and coal, together with the valley routes to the triple city of Hankau-Hanyang-Wuchang, has developed large iron-works at Hanyang.

Roads are everywhere bad. The greater amount of trade is done by canals and rivers. The Hoang-ho is

Principal street, Peking

swift and in places shallow, and is unsuitable for navigation. The Yang-tse-kiang is navigable for ocean-going steamers as far as Hankau, a three days journey inland, and for small steamers to 1000 miles inland. Its chief tributaries also are navigable. The Si-kiang is navigable for a great part of its course. Over 6000 miles of railroad are now open to traffic, and nearly half as much is under construction. Peking, the northern capital, is connected by rail with Manchuria, with the Yang-tse-kiang ports of Hankau, Nanking, and Shanghai, and with the Si-kiang ports of Canton and Kowloon (for Hong-kong).

The total foreign trade exceeds £270,000,000, the chief exports being raw and manufactured silk, beans, raw cotton, and tea. The chief imports are cotton goods. The chief ports are *Shanghai, Hankau, Canton, Tientsin, Hong-kong* (which, with the opposite Kowloon territory, is British), and *Kiao-chau* (Japanese).

Administration and Towns.

The republic is governed by a president, senate, and house of representatives. *Peking* is the capital, and *Tientsin* its port. *Canton* is the chief port of the south, and *Sianfu* the chief town in the west of the fertile Hoang-ho plain. *Shanghai* and *Hankau* have cotton and silk industries. *Fuchau* is the centre of the tea plantations.

South-Eastern Asia.

Position, Size, and Surface.

South-eastern Asia lies south of the Tropic of Cancer, and stretches as far south as parallel 10° S. It includes French Indo-China (Tonking, Annam, Cambodia, and Cochin China), Siam, the British territories (Straits Settlements, the Federated Malay States, Sarawak,

Brunei and British North Borneo), the Dutch East Indies (Java, and Madura, Sumatra, Banka and Billiton, South Borneo, Celebes, the Molucca and other islands), and the United States territory of the Philippine Islands.

The British territory is as large as the United Kingdom, the Philippines the same size, Siam half as large again, French Indo-China twice as large, and the Dutch East Indies six times as large as the British Isles. Practically all the islands except Borneo contain volcanic cones, these being especially numerous in Java. The Malay peninsula is mountainous, and is traversed by the large Mekong, rising in Tibet, and the smaller Song-ko and Menam rivers, all of which have created fertile deltas of rich, muddy sediments. The eastern part of Sumatra is lowland, as also are the southern parts of Borneo.

Climate and Natural Productions.

All places have high air-temperatures, with very hot long summers in the north, and two summer seasons in the equatorial belts. The south-west monsoons of summer bring heavy rains on the western sides of the peninsula and the islands, while the north-east winter monsoons bring rain to the eastern sides. Thus the islands receive rain at all seasons, Siam rain in summer, and Annam rain in winter. Typhoons are common in the China Sea and cause shipwrecks and other disasters.

Vegetation is everywhere luxuriant. The hilly regions are forested and teak and other hardwoods are cut and floated down stream, especially in the peninsular highlands. Rice is cultivated wherever a sufficient stretch of level land can be cleared or artificially created. Palms, such as the sago and coco-nut, are typical products of these lands; and in the islands various spices such as pepper, cloves, nutmegs, and mace, are important products. During the last few years, india-rubber and cinchona plants have been introduced into south-eastern Asia. Large amounts of coffee are produced, and exported to Amsterdam.

South-eastern Asia is occupied by many wild animals. Fish abound in the seas, and there are numerous pearl fisheries. The mineral wealth is very great. *Tin* is the chief ore mined, the annual output being about half that of the whole world. The chief tin-producing districts are the Federated Malay States, and the islands of Banka and Billiton. There are also large *coal*fields and *oil*-districts in south-eastern Asia.

People, Industries, and Commerce.

The chief inhabitants are Malays, Chinese, and Indians. Estimated at 70 millions, the population is

Native market, Java

settled mainly in the food-producing valleys. The majority of the people are Buddhists and Mohammedans.

There are few industries other than mining, agriculture, and forestry. Railways are being laid to the interior. The chief exports are tin, rice, teak, rubber, cinchona, sugar and vegetable products. Manufactured goods are the chief imports.

Administration and Towns.

Siam is governed by a King, assisted by forty ministers of state. The British territories are Straits Settlements (Singapore, Labuan, Penang, Province Wellesley, and Malacca), the Federated Malay States, Brunei, and Sarawak. British North Borneo is under the control of a British company. French Indo-China is under a governor-general, and the Dutch East Indies are also governed by a governor-general.

The chief towns are also the chief ports. *Singapore*, on Singapore Island, is a free British port and a coaling station. *Manila* is a calling place for large steamers, and exports hemp, copra, sugar, and tobacco. *Bangkok*, the Siamese capital, exports £10,000,000 worth of rice annually. *Batavia*, the Dutch port, sends most of its exports to the Netherlands.

India.

Position and Size.

India occupies the central peninsula of southern Asia. It is widest in its northern part, and tapers southward to Cape Comorin, and to the detached island of Ceylon. In the south-east, India occupies the west part of the Malay peninsula as far south as parallel 10° N. British India is nine times, and the Native States of India are nearly six times, as large as the British Isles. Ceylon is one-fifth of the size of our islands.

Surface and General Features.

India is bounded on the north by the edges of high plateaux—the Sulaiman, Pamir, and Himalayan Mts. the latter mountains stretching for over 1000 miles eastward, and containing Mt Everest, 29,000 ft. above sea-level. These mountains fall by steep slopes to two great valleys, the Indus on the west, and the Ganges on the east. The Indus river rises in the Tibet plateau, and receives the Kabul river from Iran. The joint river flows southward to a deltaic mouth north of the Tropic of Cancer, receiving on its east bank four large rivers from the Himalayas. The Indus basin north of parallel 29° N. is therefore called the Panjab, or 'Land of the Five Rivers.' The Ganges system of rivers is chiefly fed from the Himalayas. The most westerly of the large tributaries is the Jumna which receives the Chambal from the south and joins the Ganges at meridian 82° E. The Gumti and Gogra flow into the main stream from the north and the Son from the south. The Ganges turns south, after receiving several tributaries from the highest parts of the Himalayas. South of parallel 25° S. the Ganges has formed a large delta, which reaches to nearly 2° south of the Tropic of Cancer. The swampy, island part of the delta is known as the Sandarbans, and the most navigable channel is the Hugli, in the west. Into the eastern part of this delta flows the mighty river Brahmaputra.

Upper and lower Burma occupy the west part of the Malay peninsula, which is here cut into three mountainous parts by the Irawadi and Salwen. The Irawadi, after crossing the 500 ft. contour line, flows through 10° of latitude before it reaches mean sea-level. It has a large delta at its mouth.

South of the Tropic of Cancer lies the Dekkan plateau. From the western Malabar coast a steep slope known as the Western Ghats leads upward from a narrow coastal strip to the highest parts of the Dekkan plateau. From the top of these Ghats the plateau slopes gently eastward to a wider coastal plain. The northern part of the plateau slopes to the Indus-Ganges valley. Its highest part, called the Vindhya Mts, is separated from the Satpura range by the Narbada river, while south of the Satpura range the short Tapti flows parallel to the Narbada, each entering the Gulf of Cambay.

These two rivers form the only important gaps that exist in the Western Ghats, and their valleys are valuable routes into the Dekkan from the west. The gentler eastern slopes of the plateau are drained by the Mahanadi, Godavari, Kistna, and Kaveri, which have at their mouths rich deltaic lowlands. About parallel 11° N. the Western Ghats rise to the Nilgiri hills, while immediately south there is a saddle, the Palghat. The shallow Palk Strait, crossed by the rocky Adam's Bridge, connects the Coromandel coast with the north end of Ceylon. This island has a central mountain region, surrounded on all sides by a plain, which is most extensive in the north.

Climate.

Air-temperatures are at their lowest in India at the beginning of the year. The winters of the northern plains have air-temperatures like those of our summers. Temperatures rise in a southerly direction. North-west India has the highest air-temperatures in summer, and there is a gradual fall in temperature in a south-easterly direction. Equable air-temperatures are recorded near the coast, conditions becoming more extreme in the plains, and especially in the higher parts of the country.

During the winter months, India is under the influence of the north-east monsoon, which sheds rain only where its air has passed over seas. Ceylon and the southern part of the Coromandel coast receive their chief rains at this season. When the south-west monsoon blows (approximately from June to October), India receives its heaviest rains. The Western Ghats receive very heavy falls; the Dekkan, which lies to leeward, has less rain. Heavy rains fall in the north-east, especially on the southern slopes of the Himalayas and the mountains of Assam. The high southern edge of the Tibet Plateau turns some of the winds to the north-west, and so rains are shed throughout the Ganges valley. Much less rain falls in the Panjab, while east of the lower

9—2

Indus the rainfall is so low and the air-temperatures so high that the great Thar desert is formed.

Plants and Animals.

The heavy summer rainfall and the great heat are most favourable to the growth of trees. Much of the forest land has been cleared, but the well-watered slopes of the Western Ghats, Himalayas, Assam, and

A village in the Himalayas

Burma are still densely forested, and produce teak, sal, ebony, sandalwood, bamboo, and coco-nut palm. In the swampy, hot deltas, jute and other fibres grow in the clearings of the forest. The lower slopes of the Himalayas are covered by thick vegetation, forming the unhealthy jungle.

The tiger and panther roam through the forested regions, destroying thousands of lives annually. The elephant, rhinoceros, and other large wild animals are numerous, along with poisonous snakes and other reptiles. Cattle are important, not only for their milk, but as draught animals. Camels and elephants are used for similar purposes, the former in the deserts, the latter in Assam and Burma. Sheep are fed on the hill pastures for their wool.

Agriculture.

Two-thirds of the people of India are occupied in agriculture proper, and only 1 % in pastoral industries. Nearly one-sixth of the area of British India is cultivated with millet and chick-peas, which form a great part of the native food. Rice is cultivated on one-ninth of the area, chiefly in the well-watered plains. These crops, sown in June or later, at the beginning of the wet monsoon season, are reaped about six months later. North of parallel 20° N. wheat, sown in September or later, is grown in the irrigated districts of the Panjab and the upper Ganges valleys for export. Cotton is grown on the Dekkan valley slopes, especially round the Tapti. Jute is an important product of the lower Ganges; and indigo and tobacco are grown in various parts. Sugar-cane is grown in the upper Ganges and in the south-east of the Dekkan. Tea is important in the hills of Assam, East Bengal, and in Ceylon; coffee in the south-east of the Dekkan and in Ceylon; and cacao in Ceylon. Coco-nut and rubber plantations are also of great value in Ceylon.

Minerals.

Coal occurs in scattered fields, but the annual output of 12 million tons has to be supplemented by coal imported from the British Isles, Japan, and elsewhere. The chief coalfields are near *Raniganj* (long. 82° E.; lat. 23½° N.), and near the divide between the Son and Narbada. *Gold, iron, copper, tin,* and *salt* are also mined. Ceylon is noted for *graphite* and *gem-stones.*

People, Industries, and Communications.

The original inhabitants of India, now few in number, and inhabiting isolated valleys in the Dekkan, were in early times pushed southward by Aryan tribes, advancing eastward into the Panjab. These white races of agricultural people developed the land which they occupied, and are now the chief races of north India. A later invasion of Mongols from the high plateaux led to the introduction of Yellow tribes into the east of the northern plains. The people now number over 350 millions, one-fifth of these being in the Native States. The average number of people to every square mile is 175, with 578 to the square mile in the upper Ganges valley, and 52 to the square mile in Burma. Two-thirds of the people profess some form of the Hindu religion; 20 % are Mohammedans; over 3 % are Buddhists: and 1 % Christians. In Ceylon, there are 4½ million people, the majority being Buddhists.

Metal-working, wood-carving, weaving of wool, and other native industries are now of little value. Mills, worked on European lines, are increasing in number; and there are many cotton, jute, paper and wool mills.

The greater part of the carriage of goods is now done by the railways, which have been laid along the Ganges and other valleys by the British government. From Bombay lines run northward and eastward into the Jumna valley to Delhi, and north-east over the Ghats and the Dekkan to Allahabad and the Ganges valley. From this valley the railway runs into the Panjab passing through Lahore to Peshawar, the military centre commanding the Kabul valley in the north-west.

Commerce and Ports.

The total annual trade is valued at over £290,000,000, three-fifths of which represent India's exports. Two-thirds of the imports are manufactured goods, and only 5 % raw materials. Of the exports one-third are manufactured goods, one-third raw materials, and nearly one-fourth food-stuffs. Of the imported goods, the chief are cotton- and metal-manufactures; and of the exports, the chief are raw cotton, jute, rice, wheat, tea and oil-seeds. The chief exports from Ceylon are tea, rubber, coco-nut oil, and copra.

Cotton Green, Bombay

Calcutta and *Bombay* are the chief ports. *Karachi, Rangoon,* and *Madras* also are important. Some of the trade of India is carried overland by caravans.

Administration and Towns.

The Viceroy, or Governor-General, of India is appointed by the British Crown, and he has supreme authority in India. The Secretary of State for India, who is the head of the India Office, London, is entrusted with the administration of the empire in England. Assisting the governor-general in India there are a Council of State, and a Legislative Assembly. In nearly all the Native States there are British residents, or agents. Ceylon is a separate colony, with its own Governor, executive, and legislative councils.

The capital of British India is *Delhi* (population 250,000), an important railway centre. *Calcutta*, on the navigable Hugli, has over a million inhabitants, and it has jute and cotton mills and iron-works. *Bombay*, on an island off the Malabar coast, is the chief port for western trade, exporting cotton and itself having cotton mills. *Madras* has an artificial harbour and exports coffee and cotton. *Rangoon* is the chief port of lower Burma, exporting rice and teak. *Lahore* is the capital of the Panjab. *Benares*, *Agra*, and *Allahabad* are large towns in the upper Ganges basin. *Mandalay* is the old capital of upper Burma. In the Native States of India the chief towns are *Hyderabad* (half a million inhabitants), the capital of the most populous native state; *Bangalore*, the largest town in Mysore, near the productive goldfield of Kolar; and *Jaipur*, the chief town of the dozen Rajputana states. The chief town of Ceylon, *Colombo*, with over 200,000 inhabitants, does most of the trade of the island.

The Countries of the Western Plateaux.

Position, Size, and Surface.

Stretching from the Pamir plateau through nearly 50° of longitude, and from the Black and Caspian Seas on the north to the various bays of the Indian Ocean on the south, Western Asia consists of great plateaux and valleys. From the Pamirs the plateau widens and decreases in altitude. It includes many salt lakes. From the northern boundary ranges many short, swift rivers flow north. The southern mountain barrier of the plateau is deeply cut into by the Euphrates and Tigris rivers, whose lower basin forms the fertile district of Mesopotamia. This continues into the shallow Persian Gulf. South of this deep rift lies the Arabian plateau, highest on the west. In Syria, this plateau is crossed by a north—south trough occupied by the R. Jordan and the Dead Sea.

Turkey-in-Asia, about as large as the British Isles, Armenia, Syria, and Mesopotamia about the same size, and Palestine less than one-tenth this size; Arabia ten times, Persia five times, and Afghanistan twice, the size of the British Isles, are the chief political divisions of these lands.

Climate and Natural Productions.

The air-temperatures of Arabia are as high as those of northern India in summer time, and these temperatures decrease slowly in a northerly direction. The high altitudes in the west and south-west of Arabia, and generally throughout the northern plateaux, cause cooler weather in these parts. In winter, air-temperatures vary from those of the Mediterranean lands to those of Ceylon. Southern Arabia has a fair rainfall in summer; elsewhere, summer is the dry season. The northern lands, Asia Minor, Syria and Palestine, Armenia, and western Persia, receive winter rains, the amount of which decreases rapidly from west to east. Thus the climate passes from a Mediterranean type in the west to the desert type in Southern Persia, and Mesopotamia, and in Arabia. Agriculture can only be carried on where there is sufficient rainfall, or where the land can be irrigated.

In most parts there is fertile soil—except in the heart of Arabia. Wheat, vine, mulberry, tobacco, and cotton are cultivated in those districts which receive sufficient rainfall. Dates form an important food in the drier parts. The greater part of the country is pastoral land, on which goats, sheep, horses, and camels are reared.

Coal, oil, iron, and *precious metals* outcrop in Persia and Turkey-in-Asia. There are pearl fisheries in the Persian Gulf.

The People.

The majority of the people are Mohammedans and of the White race. The northern parts of the plateau are peopled by the Yellow race. It is estimated that over 4 million people live in these four countries,

Travelling in Persia

there being about 6 millions in Afghanistan, about 9 in Persia, 3 in Syria, 5 in Arabia, 3 in Mesopotamia, 0ʻ6 in Palestine and the remainder about equally between Turkey and Armenia.

Industries, Communications, and Commerce.

The pastoral industry is everywhere important, and from it has arisen the woollen industry. Persian and Turkish carpets are renowned. There are silk, woollen, and cotton factories in Syria.

Communication is everywhere difficult. The Kabul river, running from Afghanistan to the Indus, provides a valley route to the Panjab, but in one part its valley is so tortuous and narrow that a neighbouring saddle, the Khaibar Pass, is used. This pass is defended on the east by the British military town of Peshawar in India. Afghanistan is the meeting-place of routes from Persia, Russia and Chinese Turkestan, British Baluchistan, and India. Caravans following the easier routes in all the countries are now being supplanted by railways. Ocean-going steamers can reach Basra, and river steamers can go as far as Bagdad.

The chief exports of Turkey-in-Asia are silk, coffee, and figs, and the chief imports manufactured goods. *Smyrna* is the chief port. This port together with a 'hinterland' of about 5000 square miles, is administered by Greece under Turkish sovereignty. From Mesopotamia dates are the chief product, and *Basra* is the chief port of the district. Persian commerce includes among its exports cotton, fruits, and woollen goods (including carpets and raw wool), and among its imports cotton goods and sugar. The chief Caspian port is *Enzeli*, the port of Resht; and the chief gulf ports are *Bushire* and *Bandar Abbas*. Arabia has five large ports, *Jedda*, *Hodeida*, *Muskat*, and *Koweit* (independent), and *Aden* (a British coaling station). The chief Arabian exports are coffee, dates, and other fruits. *Jaffa* is the port of Jerusalem.

Administration and Towns.

Turkey-in-Asia is governed by the Sultan and a parliament. Persia is governed by the Shah and a national council. Afghanistan is governed by an Amir and four governors. Arabia is more or less independent. Hejas became an independent kingdom in 1916. Syria is governed by the French; Mesopotamia and Palestine by the British. Armenia is an independent republic.

Smyrna (population 350,000) is the chief port of Asia Minor. *Damascus*, in Syria, is of the same size;

Damascus

and *Aleppo*, north of Damascus, is the starting point of the railway, passing through Damascus, to which a branch runs from the Syrian port of *Beirut*. *Bagdad* is the largest town in Mesopotamia. *Mecca*, the birth-place of Mohammed, is twice the size of *Medina*. *Erzerum* is the chief town of Armenia.

The largest Persian towns are *Teheran* (with a quarter of a million people), the capital, *Tabriz*, the centre of the carpet industry, and *Ispahan*, a commercial town between Teheran and the Persian Gulf.

Kabul is the capital and chief town of Afghanistan. *Muskat* is the chief town of Arabia.

CHAPTER VI

AFRICA

Position and Size.

The south-west portion of the greatest 'dry' land mass in the World is known as Africa. The sandy, narrow isthmus of Suez connects Africa with Asia; the Mediterranean Sea and its narrow western mouth, the Strait of Gibraltar, separate it from the northern continent of Europe. The Red Sea and Strait of Bab-el-Mandeb separate Africa from the eastern continent of Asia. It is washed on the west by the Atlantic Ocean, and on the east by the Indian Ocean. The continent of Africa is about 95 times the size of the British Isles.

Surface and General Features.

North of parallel 5° N. Africa consists of a wide country, and south of this parallel the continent has on the average only half the width of the northern part. The wide northern part has, generally, an elevation less than 3000 ft., and the narrowing southern part is generally above that altitude, being in many parts more than 6000 ft.

The extreme north-western part of the continent is occupied by the Atlas Mts, which run S.W.—N.E. The highest parts of these mountains are in the south-west. Except for the Atlas, Africa is a continent of plateaux. The bounding ranges are higher than the interior parts of the plateaux, but they generally run parallel to the coast. From Abyssinia southward to the Province of the Cape of Good Hope there is a fairly continuous plateau edge, with a narrow coastal lowland. The African plateau, stretching to the west coast, is in its northern part occupied by the basin of the Congo, the greater part of which is less than 3000 ft. in altitude. The plateau rises north-west of the Congo to the mountainous edge of Kamerun.

The eastern limit of the Congo basin, roughly along meridian 30° E., is a deep trough with a general north—south direction. This is bordered on the east by a high plateau above which rise several mountains, such as Ruwenzori, and several volcanic cones. About 6° east of this trough, the plateau again sinks rapidly to a deep north—south trough occupied by lakes and bordered on the east by steep slopes above which tower volcanic cones, the chief being Kenya and Kilima Njaro. This eastern trough appears to pass through the Abyssinian plateau on the north, and towards the Zambesi in the south.

The wide northern part of Africa contains in the south-west the Futa Jallon highlands, and in the centre a high plateau, running N.W.—S.E. It has much wider coastal lowlands than has South Africa.

Rivers and Lakes.

From the interior of the plateaux large rivers flow to the sea, everywhere experiencing great difficulty in crossing the rims of the plateaux, at which places their courses are interrupted by cataracts and rapids. Where they have succeeded in traversing the rims, they have formed valuable gaps; and where they have not found a way through the rims, regions of inland drainage have been formed, such as Lakes Chad and Ngami, and the shotts of the Atlas plateau.

The high plateau stretching for about 10° on either side of the Equator and between meridians 30° E. and 40° E. is a region of great lakes, which feed the longest African rivers. The wonderful troughs (or rifts) occurring in this high plateau are occupied by long, deep, and narrow lakes. Those in the western trough are Lakes Albert, Edward, Kivu, and Tanganyika. In the eastern trough the chief lake is Rudolf (a salt lake). The greater part of the high plateau between the two troughs is occupied by Lake Victoria, which is 2° in width from west to east and a little more than 2° from north to south. This lake empties over the Ripon Falls in the north, giving rise to the Victoria Nile. In the Abyssinian plateau, Lake Tsana, a small lake in many ways like L. Victoria, gives rise to the Blue Nile.

The Nile, flowing northward, receives large perennial supplies of water from L. Victoria. The water from this lake runs north and west, and over the Murchison Falls to L. Albert (which also receives the waters of L. Edward through the Semliki river). The White Nile, after leaving L. Albert, flows northward, receiving the Bahr-el-Ghazal from the west, and the Sobat, Blue Nile, and Atbara from the Abyssinian plateau on the east. These eastern rivers supply large volumes of water to the White Nile during the summer months, when south winds bring rain to Abyssinia. Between the junctions of the Blue Nile and Atbara the Nile is obstructed by a waterfall or cataract, and five others occur further down stream, the last—called the first—cataract over which the Nile flows being north of the Tropic of Cancer and south of Aswan. After receiving the Atbara, the Nile flows northward without receiving any other tributaries, and north of parallel 30° N. it forms a triangular area, or delta, covered by fine deposits and intersected by numerous streams distributing water from the main stream.

The Congo flowing westward drains several lakes in the western trough of the equatorial plateau, together with Lakes Mweru and Banguelo. The main stream, when crossing the Equator on its northward journey, is interrupted by the Stanley Falls, and all its large tributaries are similarly interrupted by falls. The Congo widens in places to 10 miles, forming a long lake with a very wide portion at Stanley Pool, on the eastern side of the plateau rim. Leaving this lake the river passes through a wide gap and over many falls. Its mouth is not choked with sediment, and its fresh water can be found running many miles out to sea.

The Niger, rising in the Futa Jallon highlands, flows north-east into the Sahara desert, turning to the south-east some miles beyond Timbuktu, and receiving the Benue from the east. Its mouth is a huge delta, marshy in places, but largely covered with dense mangrove

The Victoria Falls of the Zambesi

woods. The Niger is navigable as far up stream as where it crosses meridian 5° E.

In the southern plateau of Africa the chief river is the Zambesi, which at its most southern point is interrupted by the Victoria Falls, over one mile wide, and more than twice as deep as the Niagara Falls. Near its delta, the Zambesi receives from the north the Shiré river, draining Lake Nyasa. South of the Zambesi runs the Limpopo, and further south the Orange and its tributary the Vaal drain the plateau westward to the South Atlantic Ocean.

Coasts and Islands.

The continent of Africa has less coastline than any of the other four continents. Fjords are practically absent, and the coast is remarkably regular. From the Strait of Gibraltar to Cape Verde there is practically no good harbour. From C. Verde to C. Palmas the coast is more indented; and from C. Palmas to C. Lopez the coast of the Gulf of Guinea is shallow and surf-beaten. The Niger delta separates the Bight of Benin from the Bight of Biafra, in which occur Fernando Po, St Thomas, and other islands. From C. Lopez to the Cape of Good Hope, the best harbour is the British territory of Walfish Bay. There is a good harbour at Table Bay. Algoa Bay and Durban are also good harbours in the Union of South Africa. The east coast is more indented than the west coast and it is separated by the Mozambique Channel from Madagascar. Delagoa Bay and the Chinde mouth of the Zambesi are important natural openings, and C. Guardafui is the most easterly point of this coast. The Gulf of Aden, Strait of Bab-el-Mandeb, and the coral-studded Red Sea, separating Asia from Africa, lead up to the Gulf of Suez, from the north end of which the great Suez Canal has been cut through sandy wastes and salt lakes to the Mediterranean Sea. The coast of this sea, as far west as Tunis, is low and sandy; but where the Atlas Mts run out to sea a rocky coast exists.

The largest island belonging to Africa is Madagascar, nearly twice as large as the British Isles. Near to it lie the Seychelles, Mauritius, and Reunion; and to the north-west, near to the African coast, lie the islands of Pemba and Zanzibar. Socotra is a continuation of the Somali peninsula, and Perim Island lies in the middle of the Strait of Bab-el-Mandeb. The chief islands off the west coast are volcanic cones, and include the Azores (west of the Iberian peninsula), Madeira, the Canaries, Cape Verde Is., Ascension, and St Helena.

Climate.

(a) Air-temperatures.

The greater part of Africa lies between the Tropics of Cancer and Capricorn. All places within this tropical belt receive at noon the vertical rays of the Sun for two days in the year, when they have their summer season. Because of the revolution of the Earth, the Sun shines vertically at noon over the Tropic of Cancer at the end of June, over the Equator in September, over Capricorn in December, and again over the Equator in March. The winter seasons occur six months later than these dates.

Air-temperatures are therefore high in all parts of the tropical belt. The coolest summers are in the extreme north and south, and in the higher parts of the plateaux.

(b) Rainfall.

For some distance on either side of the Equator heavy rains fall at all seasons. To the north and south of this belt, summer is the wet season. Each tropic passes through a desert. The northern Sahara desert is more extensive than the southern Kalahari desert. To the east of the Sahara there is the arid country of Arabia; but to the east of the Kalahari there is a region of heavy summer rains. In the extreme north-west and south-west of Africa rains fall chiefly in the winter months.

Plants.

The decrease in amount of rainfall going southward from the north coast of Africa and northward from the south coast, and the increasing air-temperatures, cause the vegetation to alter from perennial to annual in character, trees giving place to grasses. In the desert

areas of Sahara and Kalahari plants grow luxuriantly
after the slightest showers, but they do not live long.
On the other hand, where water oozes out of the ground
near the outcrop of porous rocks underlain by non-

Oasis in the Sahara

porous strata, longer life is possible, especially for trees
such as the date-palm, which flourishes in groves in the
spring-watered areas, or oases.

On the equatorial side of these dry deserts, grasses
grow during the wet season; and with the increase in

the amount of rain, small clusters of trees appear, until the whole country looks like a park. These *park-lands* or *savanas* gradually merge into forests nearer the Equator. For about 10° on either side of the prime parallel there are dense forests, except where the high Lake plateau occupying Uganda, the western portion of Tanganyika territory, and Northern Rhodesia interrupts this forest because of lower air-temperatures. The chief trees of the forest belt are the oil-palm, the rubber tree, mahogany, teak, and ebony. Many native foodstuffs are obtained from the trees of this belt, the chief being coffee, bananas, and ground nuts ('monkey nuts').

The savana belt may be regarded as extending in horse-shoe form, with a breadth of about 10°, from the west coast of Africa towards Abyssinia, southward through the Lake plateau, and westward across the upper Zambesi to Portuguese West Africa.

South-east Africa, receiving its rain during the time of greatest heat, produces sugar, maize, and tea. South-west and north-west Africa, having winter rains, are suited to the cultivation of Mediterranean fruits and cereals. All these regions are separated from the dry deserts by steppes, which become 'scrub' lands as the rainfall decreases.

Animals.

From the tropical forests to the desert margin, Africa is plentifully supplied with food for large numbers of wild animals. This continent is pre-eminently the home of the large flesh-eating animals, such as the lion, leopard, and hyena which feed on the antelopes, which roam over the savanas. The giraffe and zebra are also numerous in the hot grass lands, together with rhinoceros, hippopotamus, and elephant; and the camel is invaluable in the desert lands as a beast of burden. The forests are in most places so impenetrable that animal life is only possible in the tree tops; and consequently monkeys, apes, and other tree-climbers are characteristic of these regions.

The python and many other deadly snakes infest the rank undergrowth of these forests. Birds are numerous in the forests, and in the savanas. The ostrich is very important in South Africa, both in the steppes and savanas.

Minerals.

More than one-third of the World's annual *gold* output is produced from the mines in the Province of the Transvaal, especially near Johannesburg. There are also small gold-mining industries in Rhodesia, and in West Africa. *Diamonds* are exported from the mines of South Africa, and especially from the Kimberley district. *Coal* outcrops, and is mined, in the Union of South Africa, Rhodesia and Nigeria. *Copper* is produced from mines in the south-east of the Belgian Congo, in the north-west of the Cape Province and in the Protectorate of S.W. Africa; *tin* in the Province of the Transvaal and in Nigeria.

Administration.

About 39% of Africa is under the administration of the British, and 34% under French rule. Nearly 9% is Portuguese, over 8% Belgian, 5% Italian, and 1% Spanish.

Abyssinia occupies 3% of Africa, and is independent. It is governed by an Empress and council of ministers. The Liberian Republic has a President, senate and house of representatives, and the official language of the republic is English.

French Africa.

Position, Size, and General Features.

French Africa stretches from the Mediterranean Sea southwards to the Congo. The western boundary is the Atlantic Ocean, and the territories stretch more than half way eastward across North Africa. These territories are 30 times the size of the British Isles, and include Tunis, Algeria, Sahara, Mauritania, Senegal, Upper Senegal and Niger Colony, French Guinea, Ivory Coast, Dahomey, French Congo, Madagascar and neighbouring islands, and part of the Somali coast. The Atlas Mts occupy the north-west, the interior is a low plateau, and the south is drained by the Senegal, Niger, the Lake Chad inland drainage system, and the Congo. Madagascar is a mountainous island. Morocco is a French protectorate. The greater part of the former German territories of Togoland and Kamerun is now under French administration.

Climate and Natural Productions.

The northern countries—often called the Barbary States—have a Mediterranean climate; the Sahara is a region of deficient summer rainfall; the Guinea territories and equatorial Africa have heavy summer rainfall; Madagascar is for the most part a tropical island having heavy rains in both winter and summer.

The Barbary States, owing to their varied elevation, are not very productive. Wine, fruits, and cereals are grown near the coast, and much of the higher land is used for the pasture of sheep and goats. There is great mineral wealth, as yet undeveloped. The Sahara produces nothing; but the Guinea territories have valuable forests of rubber and palm trees, and hardwoods, together with important pastoral lands on their northern margins. The French Congo has large forests, producing oil and rubber, and Madagascar has valuable pastures, and exports rice, rubber, and gold.

Algiers

People, Commerce, and Ports.

The native people of the Barbary States are Berbers and Arabs, the majority of whom are Mohammedans. Under the rule of the French, colonisation by French people is taking place in various parts. The northern tropical territories are chiefly peopled by negroes, the majority of whom are pagans. Madagascar is peopled by a Malay race, who have been largely Christianised. It is estimated that there are 33 million people in French Africa.

The French have, during their rule, laid railway lines along the coastal lowland of the Barbary States, from Tunis to Algiers and to Morocco. A railway connects the valley of the Senegal with that of the Niger, and another line connects the upper Niger to the Guinea coast at Konakry. The chief east coast port of Madagascar, *Tamatave*, is connected by rail with the highland capital of *Antananarivo*. Everywhere rivers are important, and much trade is done by camel caravans across the hot, dry interiors. The total trade of French Africa is valued at over £120,000,000 annually. Fruits, oils, rubber, and hardwoods are the chief exports; and cottons, clothing, machinery and metal work, and coal, are the chief imports. *Tunis*, *Algiers* (the great coaling station of the Mediterranean), *Tangiers*, and *Mogador* are the chief northern ports; *Dakar*, *Konakry*, and *Libreville* the western ports of the tropical territories. *Jibuti*, the port of the French Somali coast, does much of the trade of Abyssinia, because of the railway leading from that port to the interior. *Duala* is the chief port of Kamerun.

Administration and Towns.

Each territory has a Governor, assisted in some cases by councils. The large towns are nearly all ports. Of the other large towns, *Fez* is the capital of Morocco, and *Morocco City* is the southern capital of the same country. *Brazzaville* is the capital of the 'Middle Congo Colony,' and is situated on the north side of Stanley Pool.

British Africa

(excluding Egypt and the Anglo-Egyptian Sudan).

Position and Size.

There are three distinct districts in the mainland of Africa under British control. More than half this British territory lies south of parallel 8° S., and stretches to the most southerly part of Africa. This territory—which we may refer to as British South Africa—includes Nyasaland, Rhodesia, the Union of South Africa, Swaziland, Basutoland, Bechuanaland, and the Protectorate of South West Africa (late German territory). The West African territories lie north of the Equator, and are best developed along the Guinea coast, the interior highlands being mostly undeveloped. In this district lie Nigeria, Gold Coast Colony, Ashanti and the Northern Territory, Sierra Leone, and Gambia. The third district occupies the high lake-studded plateau between parallels 5° N. and 10° S., and it stretches from meridian 30° E. to the east coast. Kenya Colony and Protectorate, the Uganda Protectorate, and Tanganyika Territory (formerly German East Africa) are the chief political divisions of this district. British Somaliland, on the south side of the Gulf of Aden, may be considered along with this district. The islands included in the British Empire are Ascension and St Helena, far out in the South Atlantic Ocean; Mauritius and its neighbours off the east coast of Madagascar; Zanzibar, near the coast of German East Africa; and the Seychelle Is., 16° east of Kenya Protectorate.

British Africa is 24 times, and the Union of South Africa nearly four times, the size of the British Isles.

Surface and General Features.

British Africa, south of parallel 10° S., is largely plateau. Its rim, running parallel to the coast, starts near Lake Nyasa under the name of the Livingstone range, and is continued southward under the names Matoppo range, Drakenberg, Stormberg, and the Nieuwveld range. From this last-named range several other ranges run north-west, parallel to the coast of the South Atlantic Ocean. Four steps are recognisable in the Province of the Cape of Good Hope, with three mountainous edges separating these steps. The widest and highest step—part of the high plateau—is generally known as the *veld*; the next, lower plateau is the *Great Karroo*; at a lower elevation comes the plateau, the *Little Karroo*; and the fourth, lowest step is the coastal plain. The veld is drained westward by the Orange R., and its tributaries the Caledon, Vaal, and Molopo. North of this basin, and separated from it by a divide known as the Witwatersrand, the Limpopo runs in a semi-circular course to the Indian Ocean. Rhodesia and Nyasaland are parts of the Zambesi basin, the former country containing the wonderful Victoria Falls, and the latter country L. Nyasa, which drains southward by the Shiré into the lower Zambesi. The coastal slopes of the great plateau of British South Africa are drained by many relatively short but swift rivers, nearly all of which are interrupted by waterfalls.

British West Africa contains lower plateaux than does British South Africa. Nigeria occupies the lower Niger valley and that of its tributary the Benue. The north-east of Nigeria drains to Lake Chad. Gold Coast Colony and Sierra Leone drain to the Gulf of Guinea, and Gambia is a settlement in the lower valley of the R. Gambia.

Kenya Colony and Tanganyika Territory lead upward from the east coast to the Lake plateau, which is crossed by the eastern trough near meridian 36° E. The eastern shores of L. Victoria are in Kenya Colony, the north-west shores belong to Uganda and the southern shores in Tanganyika Territory. The western boundary of Uganda is the centre of the western trough occupied by Lakes Albert and Edward and the Semliki R., and parallel 5° N. is the northern boundary of Uganda. The western boundary of Tanganyika Territory begins on the north between Lakes Kivu and Victoria. It runs south to L. Tanganyika, from the south end of this lake to the head of L. Nyasa, half way down Nyasa and then eastward along the Rovuma valley. The plateau near Kilima Njaro is the most important part of this territory. British Somaliland is a coastal plain, backed by the Abyssinian Plateau.

Climate.

British South Africa has over 15° within the Tropics, and over 11° outside this zone. The general high elevation makes the air-temperatures considerably lower than would be expected. The northern parts have a fairly equable climate, while the extreme southern parts have their summer air-temperatures modified by the indraught of cooler sea air. The south-west of the Cape of Good Hope has winter rains; Natal has heavy summer rains; and the rainfall of Orange Free State and Transvaal diminishes in a north-westerly direction. Bechuanaland (including the Kalahari Desert) is practically rainless. The rains increase north of the Kalahari, Northern Rhodesia and Nyasaland having heavy summer rainfall lasting (with intermittent dry periods) from October to April.

British West Africa has heavy summer rainfall near the coasts, rapidly decreasing in amount in the higher interior. Uganda, Kenya Colony and Tanganyika Territory have a similar climate, with two rainy seasons. Each part has very high air-temperatures.

Natural Productions.

The south-west of the Cape of Good Hope is naturally suited to the growth of citrus fruits and cereals. Natal supports large crops of maize, sugar, and tea, while the higher parts are pastoral. The rest of the Union of South Africa is essentially a pastoral country, rearing large numbers of sheep. The savanas of Rhodesia and

Nyasaland support cattle and crops of maize, cotton, coffee, and tobacco. Mauritius produces a large quantity of cane sugar, and exports it principally to the British Isles.

British West Africa is, near the coast, covered by tropical forests, which produce rubber, palm-oil, hardwoods, and cacao. The drier, higher interior is savana, and on it cotton and other valuable tropical commodities are being grown. Uganda, Kenya Colony and Tanganyika Territory have products similar to those of the west,

A diamond mine, Kimberley

Uganda producing nearly one-third of the cotton grown in the British Empire. Coffee is an important crop in the north of Tanganyika Territory.

Diamonds are mined near Kimberley in the Cape of Good Hope, and *copper* occurs in the north-west of this Province, and near Otavi in the Protectorate of Southwest Africa. In Transvaal the divide between the Limpopo and Orange basins, known as the Witwatersrand (Whitewatersridge), or 'Rand,' contains the outcrops of reefs of gold-bearing quartz. Nearly 40% of the

World's annual output of *gold* comes from these reefs, Johannesburg being the centre of the mining industry. *Coal* seams outcrop in the Middelburg district, east of the Rand; and *diamonds, petroleum, tin,* and other minerals are also worked in this Province. Natal has *coal* outcrops at Dundee, Vryheid, and other places in the north-west of the Province. Rhodesia's chief minerals are *gold*, found between Salisbury and Bulawayo, and *coal*, chiefly worked on the Wankie coalfield, about 100 miles south-east of the Victoria Falls. British West Africa produces *gold* from the Gold Coast Colony, and *tin* from the high land running along parallel 10° N. from a tributary of the Niger to a tributary of the Benue.

The People of British Africa.

The Bantus of British South Africa have during historic times displaced the dwarf Bushmen, pushing their way southward from the savanas to the steppes. Two and a half centuries ago the Dutch (now known as Boers) settled in the far south, and a decade or more later they were reinforced by settlers from France, who sought refuge in this colony from religious persecution. A century ago the Cape of Good Hope came under British rule and soon British settlers arrived in the colony. For various reasons at later periods the Boers trekked northward, forming pastoral settlements between the Orange and Limpopo rivers and also on the eastern slopes of the plateau edge in Natal. The British, after several wars with the Boers, founded in 1910 the Union of South Africa, which includes the Provinces of the Cape of Good Hope, Natal, Orange Free State, and Transvaal. The population of the Union is nearly six millions, less than a quarter of the population however being Europeans. Rhodesia, formerly inhabited by Bushmen, was during last century invaded by Zulu tribes. Over twenty years ago, the British South Africa Company, headed by Mr Cecil Rhodes, received a Royal Charter to develop the lands north of the

Limpopo. The land so developed is now divided into Southern and Northern Rhodesia by the Zambesi. Southern Rhodesia has a million inhabitants, 5% of whom are Europeans; Northern Rhodesia has nearly one million inhabitants, with just over 2000 Europeans. Nyasaland became a British Protectorate in 1891. It has about one million inhabitants, not 1000 of whom are Europeans.

Typical Boers on the Veld

British influence in West Africa dates from the reign of Queen Elizabeth, but Nigeria the largest part only became British at the end of last century. The native races are negroes except in the savanas of the north where the Fulani are a pastoral people and the Hausas the chief traders, both races being Mohammedans. The population of British West Africa is estimated at 28 millions.

Uganda and Kenya Colony, originally peopled by the Bantu tribes, early came under the influence of Arabs and Hindu traders. The Portuguese in their journeys round Africa to India made the coast ports calling stations; but the country only came under British control a quarter of a century ago. There are about 14 million natives in

Hausa warriors

Uganda, Kenya Colony and Tanganyika Territory, together with over 30,000 Asiatics, and 14,000 Europeans.

Communications.

Of the three great rivers draining British Africa, the Niger is the most navigable, and that only as far as its junction with the Benue. The Zambesi is interrupted by rapids about 150 miles after leaving Rhodesia, and the Orange is navigable only for a few miles.

All British Africa (except Gambia and the Somaliland Protectorate) is well supplied with railways. In British

South Africa the railways connect the chief mining towns with the ports. The main line of the South African railway leads from Cape Town north-east over the four steps to De Aar junction, north to Kimberley and Mafeking, and through the Bechuanaland Protectorate to Bulawayo. From Bulawayo one line crosses into Northern Rhodesia, near the Victoria Falls, and another line runs northward to Salisbury. A line runs from Salisbury eastward through Umtali to the Portuguese port of Beira. From 'Fourteen Streams,' the main line station north of the Vaal, an important line runs north-east to Johannesburg and the Witwatersrand, and thence northward to Pretoria. This district is also connected by rail with the Middelburg coalfield, and with Lourenço Marques, the chief port of Portuguese East Africa. Durban, the port of Natal, is in communication by rail with the Witwatersrand, and East London and Port Elizabeth are connected by lines running roughly parallel to the main line with the same district. There is through communication from Cape Town to Walfish Bay, in South-west Africa, and a line from that bay to Otavi.

The chief railway in British West Africa runs from Lagos, the port of Nigeria, to Jebba on the Niger, and then to Zungeru, Zaria and Kano.

The Uganda railway leads from Mombasa north-west through Nairobi the capital of the Kenya Colony to Kisumu on the east shores of L. Victoria. Large steamers sail across this lake to Entebbe, the lake port of Uganda. From Tanga, the northern port of Tanganyika Territory, a line runs north-west to the Kilima Njaro plateau; and there is also a railway from Dar-es-Salaam to Ujiji on L. Tanganyika.

Commerce and Ports.

The total annual trade of British Africa is over £140,000,000. Of this the trade of the Union of South Africa is over £80,000,000. Nearly half of the trade of British Africa is done with the Motherland.

The imports are cotton goods and apparel, machinery and hardware. Into the Union of South Africa food and drink are also imported; and living animals and chemicals are among the imports of Transvaal. From the Union of South Africa the chief exports are gold and diamonds, wool and mohair, hides and skins, coal and maize. Natal exports coal; and the exports of Orange Free State are chiefly the produce of its agricultural and pastoral industries. From Rhodesia comes gold, and some tobacco; Nyasaland exports cotton, and tobacco. The chief exports of Kenya Colony and Tanganyika Territory are copra and coffee, and of the Uganda Protectorate, cotton and coffee. Zanzibar exports cloves and copra. Palm-kernels, palm-oil, and rubber form the chief exports of British West Africa. In addition, Nigeria exports raw cotton and tin-ore, the Gold Coast Colony exports cacao, gold, and lumber, while ground nuts form three-fourths of the exports of Gambia.

The chief ports of British South Africa are *Cape Town, Port Elizabeth, East London,* and *Durban.* The chief port of Kenya Colony and Uganda is *Kilindini,* the port of Mombasa; Tanga and Dar-es-Salaam are the ports of Tanganyika Territory. *Zanzibar* is an entrepôt. The chief ports of British West Africa are *Lagos, Port Harcourt* (east of the Niger delta) and *Freetown.*

Administration.

The various colonies and protectorates of British Africa are controlled by governors, assisted by executive and legislative councils. The Uganda Protectorate is largely governed by native kings or chiefs, under the control of a British governor. Rhodesia is administered by the British South Africa Company. The Union of South Africa is ruled by a Governor-general, appointed by the King, and an executive council. The legislative power is vested in a parliament, consisting of the King (represented by the Governor-general), a Senate, and a House of Assembly. The four Provinces of the Union have also administrative and provincial councils. The Protectorate of South-west Africa is administered by the Union of South Africa.

Towns.

The meeting-place of the South African parliament is at *Cape Town*, the capital of the Cape of Good Hope, and the seat of the government of the Union is at *Pretoria*,

The Houses of Parliament, Cape Town

the capital of Transvaal. *Pietermaritzburg* and *Bloemfontein* are the capitals of Natal and Orange Free State respectively. *Kimberley, Port Elizabeth,* and *East London* are small, but important, towns in the Cape of Good Hope. *Durban* is the chief port, and *Dundee* the coal-mining centre, of Natal. *Johannesburg*, the largest town in British South Africa, is a gold-mining centre, and *Middelburg* is the coal-mining centre of Transvaal.

11—2

Southern Rhodesia's capital is *Salisbury*, and other towns are *Bulawayo*, *Victoria*, and *Umtali*. *Livingstone* is the capital of Northern Rhodesia, and *Zomba* that of Nyasaland. *Blantyre* is the chief settlement in the Shiré Highlands. *Nairobi* and *Entebbe* are the capitals of Kenya Colony and the Uganda Protectorate respectively; and *Mombasa* and *Berbera* are the ports of Kenya Colony and the Somaliland Protectorate. *Zungeru*, *Zaria*, *Lokoja*, *Kano*, and *Bauchi* are noteworthy in Northern Nigeria, while *Lagos* is the capital of Nigeria. The chief towns in the Gold Coast Colony and Protectorate are *Accra*, the capital, and *Kumasi*. *Freetown* and *Bathurst* are the capitals of Sierra Leone and Gambia, respectively.

Egypt and the Anglo-Egyptian Sudan.

Position and Surface.

That part of the Nile valley which lies north of parallel 5° N. is divided into the Anglo-Egyptian Sudan and Egypt. The total area of these countries is over 10 times that of the British Isles.

The southern part of this area is an elevated plain, bordered by the foot slopes of the equatorial and Abyssinian plateaux. The most noteworthy falls in the waters of the Nile after leaving this plain are over the six cataracts. After flowing over the 'first' cataract, the river flows uninterruptedly through a distance greater than that from Land's End to Berwick, ending its course in a delta with two navigable distributaries.

Climate.

The extreme south has two hot seasons with fairly equable air-temperatures, while north Egypt has one long, hot season and an extreme climate. Egypt is practically rainless in summer. The southern Sudan, on the other hand, receives heavy rains twice each year, and northern Sudan and Abyssinia have a long, wet summer season. The result of this distribution of the rains is that the upper White Nile floods first, the Sobat follows, the enormous Blue Nile floods come later, and the smaller Atbara floods come last down the lower Nile. At the Egyptian frontier there is, during September a flow of about 300,000 cubic feet of water every second, diminishing by the end of the

Native canoe on the Nile

following May to about 20,000 cubic feet every second. Similar conditions of the Nile occur at later dates in lower Egypt, although scarcely a drop of rain is known to fall in Egypt in summer.

In winter Egypt and the Sudan are swept by north winds, and some winter rains fall in the extreme north. The amount decreases, however, in a southward direction, Cairo for example having less than 1½ inches annual rainfall.

Natural Productions.

The southern Sudan is a savana land, and supports large herds of cattle. From the tree-clusters, which tend to become thicker in the south, gum and rubber are obtained. The huge lake, formed south of parallel 10° N. during the floods of the Sobat and Blue Nile, is in summer choked with floating masses of densely matted vegetation known as *sudd*. This when dried and compressed is used for fuel. The northern rainless districts of the Nile valley are sandy and rocky wastes, except within the limits of the Nile floods, which have been known to extend four or more miles on either side of the low water boundaries. In this strip of oasis, on either side of the Nile, plants grow luxuriantly after the floods.

The custom of the Egyptians was to plant seeds in the alluvium deposited by the stagnant water, and as this sowing time was October or later, the crops were of necessity such as could ripen with air-temperatures similar to those of the north European summer. Under the present system of perennial irrigation, it is possible in summer to grow in the Nile valley, north of Aswan, the summer crops of the Ganges valley. Cotton is the chief crop reaped in summer, along with sugar and rice; maize and millets are reaped in autumn, and wheat grows during the Nile winter.

People, Communications, and Commerce.

There are over 12 million people in Egypt, and more than 3 millions in the Anglo-Egyptian Sudan. The total Mohammedan population is over 10 millions. There are three-quarters of a million Copts, who are the traders and artisans of Lower Egypt, and a Christian people. Arabs are the chief traders in the Nile valley. In the savana lands and in the scattered oases of the Libyan desert there are many nomadic tribes, collectively known as *bedawin*.

The Nile, navigable at all seasons up to the 'First'

Cataract, is the chief route into the interior. *Alexandria,* west of the Nile delta, is the chief port of the Nile valley, over half the vessels trading there being British. Railways now follow the valley south to beyond Aswan. From Khartum government steamers carry passengers and goods as far south as the Uganda border.

The Suez Canal, a part of Egypt, is of more importance to Europe, Asia, and Australasia than to

In the Suez Canal

Africa. The canal is nearly 100 miles long, about a quarter of it passing through salt lakes. Nearly 60 % of the vessels using the canal are British.

The chief imports of Egypt and the Sudan are cotton and linen goods, machinery, and coal. The leading exports of Egypt are raw cotton and cereals. From Anglo-Egyptian Sudan, gum, ivory, ostrich feathers, and cereals are exported.

Administration and Towns.

Egypt is now a British Protectorate. It is governed by a Sultan (an Egyptian) appointed by the British Government, who is assisted by a High Commissioner (a Briton). The Anglo-Egyptian Sudan is administered by a British Governor-general.

Cairo, with nearly 800,000 inhabitants, is the capital of Egypt. West of it lie the most famous of the Egyptian pyramids. Cairo is a winter health resort for Europeans. *Alexandria* is the chief seaport, and *Port Said* the Mediterranean port of the Suez Canal. The capital of the Anglo-Egyptian Sudan is *Khartum*, and *Port Sudan* is the chief port.

Belgian Africa.

Position, Size, and Surface.

The Belgian Congo includes nearly all the basin of the Congo. Its northern boundary is the Ubangi, a tributary of the Congo. The colony extends from 5° north of, to 10° south of, the Equator. The eastern boundary lies mainly along the western trough of the Lake plateau, and in the west the colony narrows down, and occupies the wonderful Congo gap. Belgian Congo is over seven times the size of the British Isles.

The greater part of this colony is under 3000 ft. In the east the land rises rapidly to the high edge of the western trough. The southern parts of the colony are highland, but the north is low. The Congo, after passing Stanley Falls near the Equator, expands and becomes a long lake, with its greatest expansion, Stanley Pool, near the plateau rim. From it the river falls in a series of rapids to a long and deep mouth.

Climate and Natural Productions.

Air-temperatures are high and equable. Rain falls in all parts, and there are two rainy seasons. Trees flourish under such conditions, and tend to crowd out all other forms of life. The animal life is generally small in size, snakes, apes, and innumerable birds being characteristic. There are, however, large herds of elephants. Rubber is the chief product of this forest colony. Palm-nuts and oil, copal and cacao are other products. *Copper* ore is an important product of the Katanga highlands in the south-east.

People, Communications, and Towns.

The majority of the 15 million people are Bantus, but in places pigmies are met with. Most of the people are fetish worshippers.

The Congo is navigable for 100 miles inland to *Matadi*. A railway, running through the Congo gap, makes communication possible with *Leopoldville*, on the south shores of Stanley Pool. From this trading centre navigation of the river is possible for nearly 600 miles inland.

Palm-nuts and oil, copper, copal and rubber are the chief exports, and cottons, machinery, and iron goods are the chief imports. Most of the trade is carried on with Antwerp from the ports of *Boma* and *Banana*.

The King of the Belgians is represented in the colony by a Governor-general, whose capital is at *Boma*.

CHAPTER VII

AUSTRALIA AND NEW ZEALAND

Australia.

Position and Size.

The island-continent of Australia lies south-east of the greatest land-mass in the World. The area of Australia, together with the heart-shaped island of Tasmania to the south, is nearly 3,000,000 square miles—about 25 times the size of the British Isles. Papua, together with the former German territories of North-east New Guinea (late Kaiser Wilhelm Land), the Bismarck archipelago and the Solomon Islands, have a total area 1½ times that of the British Isles.

Surface and General Features.

The greater part of the land surface of Australia is under 3000 ft. On the east the land rises rapidly from the sea, attaining heights of over 3600 ft., and in the south-east the land rises to over 6000 ft. From these high parts the land slopes more gently westward. The west coast is similarly bordered by high ridges, but the slopes inland are less steep than those from the east coast. The west coastal ridge is in general the seaward edge of wide tablelands.

The East Australian highlands are a series of mountain ranges and are known by different names in various parts. In the south where they take a west—east direction, they are known as the Great Dividing Range. This leads eastward to the highest part of the highlands, the Australian Alps, which are known north of parallel 35° S. as the Blue Mts. The valley of the R. Hunter separates the Blue Mts from the Liverpool and New England Ranges. In Queensland, the highlands are generally called the Great Dividing Range. The highest peaks of the highlands are to be found in the Australian Alps, Kosciusko (7318 ft.) being the chief peak, and Townsend to the north fifty feet less in height. These peaks and the neighbouring heights are always snow-clad, the snow-field descending 600 ft. or 700 ft. downward from their summits. The lower Victoria portion of the Australian Alps is not, as a rule, snow-clad in summer.

Divides, Rivers, and Lakes.

The divides of Australia lie generally near the coast. The most clearly-marked divide runs along the Cordilleras, from Cape York in the north, parallel to the east coast, and curving round so as to run along parallel 37° 30′ S. From this divide, relatively short and swift rivers run eastward and southward to the South Pacific Ocean. The chief of these are the Burdekin, Fitzroy, Brisbane, Hunter, Snowy, Yarra Yarra, and Glenelg. The rivers running westward from the Cordilleras may be divided into three groups :

(a) Mitchell, Gilbert, Flinders, draining to the Gulf of Carpentaria,

(b) Diamantina, Cooper's Creek, and others, feeding an inland depression,

(c) The Murray basin, which is more than three times the area of the British Isles.

The chief rivers of the Murray system are the Darling, with its north bank tributary the Condamine; the Murrumbidgee, flowing within 50 miles of the Pacific Ocean, and its feeder the Lachlan; the Murray rising near the snow-clad portion of the Australian Alps; and the Goulburn, running northward from the Victorian Dividing Range to the Murray. After receiving its last great tributary at 142° E., the Murray runs for over 2° westward, then turns abruptly southward near parallel 34° S., and winding its way across the south-eastern part of South Australia, enters the large, shallow Lake Alexandrina. This lake has two eastward extensions, Lake Albert and the Coorong. Its south-western portion is occupied by several large islands. The southern boundary of the Coorong, separating it from Encounter Bay, is the Younghusband peninsula, a great bank of sand-dunes. This peninsula is separated from the western mainland by the narrow mouth of the R. Murray, a rocky opening extremely difficult to navigate because of its shallow and surf-beaten character.

The western coastal ridges of the wide plateaux shed several rivers to the Indian Ocean. Of these, the Swan, Murchison, Ashburton, Fitzroy, and Victoria are the chief.

More than half of Australia is a region of inland drainage. The south coast, between meridians 122° E. and 136° E., is nowhere crossed by a sea-going river. The depression referred to above along with a southward extension receives the internal drainage of the island continent, Lake Eyre being fed by the waters shed from the western side of the Great Dividing Range, and from the south side of the central high plateau, Torrens west of and Frome east of the Flinders range receiving rivers from that range, and Gairdner receiving tributaries from the Gawler ranges. This lake basin is separated from the Murray basin by the southern part of the Flinders range, which forms the mountainous peninsula lying between the Gulf of St Vincent and the Murray. The south-western portion of Western Australia is occupied by a number of salt lakes.

The Coast.

The northern shallow Arafura Sea, separating the Malay and Melanesian archipelagoes from Australia, extends under the name of the Gulf of Carpentaria far into the interior of Australia. The coastline of Arnhem Land is very indented and has good harbours. The coast of the Cape York peninsula is not so indented. The east coast especially south of the Tropic of Capricorn has many valuable harbours. The chief of these is Port Jackson, unsurpassed for size by any other harbour in the World. The Great Barrier Reef, built of coralline limestone, extending from Torres Strait to the Tropic of Capricorn, shelters the western mainland from heavy waves.

The south coast, from Cape Howe (150° E.) to Cape Catastrophe (136° E.), contains three large openings, Port Phillip Bay, St Vincent Gulf, and Spencer Gulf. Encounter Bay, into which the Murray empties, is surf-beaten, but its northern coast has provided sites for two ports connected by rail with the shores of L. Alexandrina. From Cape Catastrophe westward, the Great Australian Bight occupies a wide bay. The Bight is backed for a great part of its coast by cliffs, 500 ft. or more in height. King George Sound (35° S.) makes up for this inhospitable region by its large inner and outer harbours. The south-west coast is not much broken by bays, or river-mouths; but the north-western coast is much indented, and has very high tides which make navigation difficult.

Climate.

(a) Air-temperatures.

By the end of December the Sun's rays shine vertically over the Tropic of Capricorn. All places south of this parallel receive their greatest heat from the Sun at this time of the year, which is therefore their summer season. A central belt of high air-temperatures lies on either side of the Tropic, and air-temperatures diminish slowly southward. In winter (about July), there is a general increase in air-temperatures from south to north. The southern parts of the continent have winter temperatures like those of the Mediterranean lands.

(b) Rainfall.

During the Australian summer the north and north-east receive heavy rain. The Cordilleras make the rainfall greater on their windward (in this case seaward) side, and also tend to prevent the rain from being spread as far inland as would be expected. The south-western half of the continent has little chance of receiving summer rains, because the winds blowing over it are warmed as they travel northward over its flat surface. In winter southern Australia comes under the influence of rain-shedding winds. The southern part of Western Australia receives a heavy winter rainfall which diminishes in a north-easterly direction. South-east Australia also receives winter rains. These regions, therefore, have a Mediterranean type of climate.

The Murray River

Special character of Australian rivers.

The rivers draining into the lake basin, and into the Murray basin, do not receive much rain either in summer or in winter. The intense heat of the interior in summer, moreover, makes evaporation go on at a great rate and nearly all the rivers shrink enormously, becoming in some instances mere brooks, and in places disconnected pools of water. The Murray and Murrumbidgee, however, receive at this time water from the melting snows of the snow-clad Australian Alps, and are consequently perennial streams.

In *good* seasons, the Murray is navigable from Goolwa (the mainland port, west of the archipelago of Lake Alexandrina) to Albury (1366 miles); the Darling, from its junction with the Murray at Wentworth, to Walgett (1180 miles); the Murrumbidgee from Murray Junction to Narrandera (455 miles)—a total navigable distance of 3000 miles.

Plants and Animals.

Much of Australia is a region of low summer rainfall, and the native plants of the continent are nearly all adapted to live under dry conditions.

In the north, which has a hot, wet season and a warm, dry season, rubber and other tropical trees grow abundantly. Along the wetter coastal strips in the north-east there are forests of gum trees, producing the valuable hardwoods jarrah and karri. In the south-west there are also forests of hardwoods. The low, dry plains of the hot interior are covered with impenetrable growths of dwarfed gum trees bearing innumerable prickles and spines. This growth of dwarf trees—sometimes ten feet high—is known as 'scrub.' The drier parts of the interior are unable to support any vegetation and are stony wastes, or deserts.

The higher and cooler plains immediately to the west of the Cordilleras, receiving a fair supply of summer rains, are covered with grasses. The tropical parts of these plains are like the savanas of Africa, and south of the Tropic the inland side of the Cordilleras is like the steppe of eastern Europe. Both savana and steppe gradually lead inland to the drier regions of scrub and desert. There is a similar, but narrower, belt of savanas and steppes on the inland side of the west coast ranges.

The native animals of Australia are as unlike the Old World types as are the native plants. The mammals are chiefly marsupial, kangaroo, opossum and wombat being typical. Crocodiles and lizards inhabit the waters of the northern rivers, and snakes are numerous, especially in the wooded districts. Many of the birds are equally peculiar. The emu, found only in Australia, and the cassowary of north-east Australia and Melanesia are closely related to the African ostrich. Other noteworthy birds are the lyre bird, bower bird, black swan and cockatoo. Fish are abundant, in both the seas and rivers of Australia. Mackerel, herring, and whiting are caught in the seas, and cod and trout abound in the rivers. Off the north and west coasts, there are pearl fisheries, and the south-east coast has oyster beds.

Sheep crossing a temporary bridge

Agriculture and Pasture.

Since the year 1788, when Captain Phillip arrived at Botany Bay (and later at Port Jackson) with 29 sheep on board his transports, the colonists have imported special merino sheep from the Cape of Good Hope, England, and elsewhere. The breeding of sheep has gone on to such an extent, that there are now 85 million sheep in Australia, 40 millions being in New South Wales. Other valuable animals have been introduced and bred by the settlers, and there are 12 million cattle and one-fifth as many horses in the island. The plains on the inland and drier side of the Cordilleras form the chief sheep pasturage in Victoria, New South Wales, and in the southern part of Queensland. Cattle and horses are reared on the seaward and wetter sides of the Cordilleras.

The Mediterranean type of climate experienced in south-west and south-east Australia has led to the rapid development of large wheat farms, especially in Victoria. The wheat-producing area has been extended over the Cordilleras, in both Victoria and New South Wales, and there are also large areas under wheat in South Australia. Mediterranean types of fruits are also being produced in the southern parts of Australia, especially on the northern sunny slopes of the mountain ranges of Victoria. Going northward to Queensland, the higher air-temperatures and greater rainfall cause wheat to be replaced by maize. The tropical climate also allows sugar, bananas, pineapples, oranges, tobacco, and many other tropical products to be successfully cultivated.

The great drawback, both to pastoral and to agricultural industries in the interior of Australia, is the uncertainty in the amount of the rainfall. In the south of Queensland and north of New South Wales, many bore-holes, sunk into the water-bearing strata underlying the surface rocks, have tapped large stores of water; and there is now less risk of loss of stock through drought. In the Murray basin water is drawn from the rivers. In several districts dams have been built across the rivers to form huge lakes up-stream, from which the water is spread by canals over the surrounding fields. Irrigation works now exist at Renmark, Mildura and Corowa on the Murray, on the

Goulburn and other Murray tributaries in Victoria, and at Hay and Narrandera on the Murrumbidgee.

Minerals.

Australia comes third in the list of the gold-producing countries of the World. *Gold* reefs outcrop on the inland side of the Cordilleras west of Sydney, on the northern and southern slopes of the Victorian Dividing Range, and in the salt lake district of Western Australia.

Broken Hill Silver Mines

Coal is fortunately abundant.   A large coalfield extends between parallels 33° S. and 35° S. along the coast of New South Wales and inland in a north-westerly direction to beyond parallel 32° S., the chief coal-mining district being the Hunter valley.   Queensland has coal outcrops in the Brisbane valley ; and Western Australia has coal outcrops east of Geographe Bay.   *Silver* is mined in the far west of New South Wales, at Willyama (Broken Hill) and Silverton; *copper* deposits are worked in the district between the gulfs of Spencer and St Vincent; and *tin* is mined in Tasmania, Queensland and New South Wales.

Industries and Communications.

Pastoral, mining and agricultural industries are the chief means of livelihood of the people. About 10 % of the people are engaged in factories, producing clothing, metal-work, and machinery, chiefly for use in the Australian states. Wool, wheat and flour, tinned meat and butter form the chief exports.

The rivers of Australia are not generally navigable. The Murray may be made navigable in the future by locking its waters and by making a navigable channel between Lake Alexandrina and Encounter Bay. At present railways are the chief means of communication. The chief railway line runs from Sydney (the premier port of Australia), over the Blue Mountains, across the Murray basin, and over the Victorian Cordilleras to Melbourne. From Melbourne lines run north-west to Adelaide. The Trans-Australian railway, opened in 1917, continues the Adelaide—Port Augusta line westward past Lake Gairdner and across the Nullarbor plain and the Premier Downs to Kalgoorlie. Rockhampton (latitude $23\frac{1}{2}°$ S.) is connected by rail with Brisbane and Sydney. Western Australia has railways connecting the Swan River settlements with the gold-mining districts.

Administration.

From the 'mother-colony' of New South Wales all the east coast states have, from time to time, separated, Tasmania leading, New Zealand (now quite independent of the Australian government) following, while later Victoria and Queensland received responsible government. South Australia was founded from its capital, Adelaide, in 1836; and Western Australia, at first a Crown Colony, became independent in 1890. In 1901, the Commonwealth of Australia was formed, the six 'original states' being New South Wales, Victoria, Queensland, South Australia, Western Australia and Tasmania. The Commonwealth's laws are administered by a Federal Parliament, which consists of the King (represented by a Governor-general), senate, and a house of representatives. It governs a population of 5 million people. Each state has also its own parliament and governor. The Federal Parliament is to meet at *Canberra*, in the south-east of New South Wales. In addition to the six original states, the Federal Parliament now has control of the Northern Territory of Australia, and over the British part of New Guinea (Papua) and the former German territories in north-east New Guinea, the Bismarck archipelago and the Solomon Islands.

Victoria.

Position, Size, and Surface.

The south-east part of Australia is known as Victoria. This state has an area three-quarters of that of the British Isles. Its northern part, drained by the Murray and its tributaries, is wider than that occupied by the sea-slopes of the Cordilleras. The coastline is much indented, and between Cape Otway and Wilson's Promontory a wide opening leads to the natural harbour of Port Phillip Bay. The northern boundary of the state is the Murray river, the western boundary is meridian 141° E., and the eastern boundary is a line drawn from the head of the Murray river south-east to Cape Howe.

Climate and Natural Productions.

Victoria has a temperate climate, especially south of the Cordilleras. The mountainous districts have the heaviest rainfall, a yearly fall of 50 inches being common in the Alps. The rainfall decreases in amount in a westerly and north-westerly direction. In the extreme north-west of the state less than 15 inches of rain fall annually. The well-watered northern slopes of the Cordilleras are great wheat-producing belts; and where water is obtained from the Murray and its tributaries olives, grapes, apricots, and peaches are produced. The cooler southern slopes of the hills are better adapted for pastoral than for agricultural puposes. Dairy-farming is important, and butter is largely exported from the state.

Threshing wheat in Australia

On an average, 2½ millions sterling of *gold* was annually produced before the war, much of it being used at the Melbourne mint. The gold-mining centres are *Bendigo* north of, and *Ballarat* south of the Cordilleras.

Commerce and Towns.

Gold, wool, live-stock, cereals, butter, hides and frozen meat form the chief exports, while the imports are chiefly manufactured goods, such as clothing, machinery, iron and steel. The state of Victoria does over one-third of the foreign commerce of the Commonwealth, the chief port being *Melbourne*, the state capital, with a population of 700,000. The total population of the state is about twice that of its capital. Of the other towns, *Ballarat*, *Bendigo*, and *Geelong* (an outport of the capital) are noteworthy. *Mildura* is a rapidly developing irrigation colony, on the south side of the Murray. It produces raisins and currant grapes and Mediterranean types of fruits.

Tasmania.

Position, Size, and Surface.

Tasmania is a mountainous state, less than one-fourth the size of the British Isles. The plateau, which occupies all but a narrow coastal plain, is cut into western and eastern portions by the Macquarie gap. To the west of this gap lies a renowned lake district, and from these lakes rivers drain to the Derwent which empties into a fine natural harbour on the south-east coast. This island is separated from Australia by Bass Strait.

Climate and Natural Productions.

Tasmania has less heat from the Sun than any other part of the Commonwealth. The altitude of the interior gives it still lower air-temperatures, and the nearness of all places to the sea causes these air-temperatures to be modified, in both summer and winter, especially in the western part of the island. Rains fall at all seasons.

The higher parts and western parts of the island are well-wooded with gum and pine trees. Fruit trees, producing apples, pears and plums, grow to perfection in the mild climate; and oats and wheat are the chief crops. Sheep- and dairy-farming are important industries. *Tin* and *copper* are mined in the north-west; and *gold*, *silver*, and *coal* are also raised.

Commerce and Towns.

Wool, fruit, and jam, timber and minerals form the chief exports. Much of the trade is done through *Hobart*, the capital. *Launceston*, at the head of the Tamar estuary, carries on trade by rail through the Macquarie gap with its southern rival. Out of Tasmania's population of 200,000, Hobart has 40,000 and Launceston 25,000 inhabitants.

New South Wales.

Position, Size, and Surface.

From the eastern coast of the island continent, the state of New South Wales stretches westward for 10° more or less. Its southern boundary is the Murray river and its western boundary is meridian 141° E. A great part of its northern boundary is parallel 29° S. The country so enclosed has an area 2½ times that of the British Isles.

The narrow coastal plain leads to very steep slopes up the Cordilleras of New South Wales, from which gentle slopes lead westward into the Murray basin. Plains occupy the greater part of the state. The part of this district between the Murrumbidgee and the Murray is called the Riverina. In the south-east, the Riverina is bordered by the snow-capped Alps from which the Murray and Murrumbidgee receive large floods when the other streams further north are drying up.

Climate and Natural Productions.

From south to north there is always a gradual increase in the air-temperatures. The high lands of the Alps, Blue Mountains, Liverpool and New England ranges

have much lower temperatures; and the coastal belt
also has modified temperatures when it is swept by sea
breezes. Rain falls chiefly in summer and varies in
amount from 70 inches in the northern part of the
coast to 35 inches in the south coastal plain. The tablelands of the Cordilleras are well-watered, especially in
the south. The 20 inches isohyet runs roughly parallel
to the coast and 4° west of it. Half the state has a rainfall

Combined Harvester at work, N.S.W.

of less than 20 inches annually. In the far north-west the
recorded mean annual rainfall is not 10 inches.

The coast plain is a rich dairy-farming country, which
leads northward to sugar plantations east of the Richmond
range. The coastal plain between and behind Newcastle
and Sydney is a great fruit-growing district producing
oranges, lemons, peaches, apricots and grapes. In the
tableland the cooler climate makes mixed farming important; and on the western slopes of the Cordilleras

wheat is grown extensively. The great plains of the Riverina form the sheep-runs of New South Wales, supporting about 40 million sheep.

Gold is obtainable in many parts of the Cordilleras, especially on their western slopes. About £400,000 worth of gold is now produced annually, though since the discovery of the precious metal in 1851 over £60,000,000 worth of gold has been obtained. There are valuable *silver* mines near the western border of the state, at Silverton and Willyama. *Copper* and *tin* are produced in considerable amounts, and there are workable deposits of *iron* ore outcropping about 100 miles west of Sydney. *Coal* is now the most important mineral, and the coastal coalfield produces £5,000,000 worth of coal annually. The chief collieries lie in the Hunter valley, and Newcastle is the chief exporting centre. *Oil-shales* outcrop on the coalfield.

Commerce and Towns.

The exports of New South Wales are mainly wool, butter, wheat, minerals and meat. The chief imports are textile goods. From the principal port and capital, *Sydney* (population 800,000) railways lead westward over the Blue Mountains to the Riverina and Victoria, and northwards to Newcastle and to Queensland. *Newcastle* is the second port of the state. *Bathurst*, on the western slopes of the Blue Mountains, is in the centre of the wheat belt; and *Albury* is an important irrigation district on the north side of the Murray, producing raisins and other Mediterranean fruits

The total population of the state is estimated at nearly two millions.

Queensland.

Position, Size, and Surface.

The north-eastern portion of Australia, terminating in Cape York peninsula and bounded on the west by meridians 138° E. and 141° E. and parallel 26° S., forms the state of Queensland, which has an area $5\frac{1}{2}$ times the size of the British Isles. This state has physical features very similar to those of New South Wales. The Cordilleras are, however, wider and lower than their southern continuations. The parts of the western slopes of the Cordilleras, which are drained by the Condamine and Darling and which are known as the Darling Downs, form the healthiest part of Queensland.

Climate and Natural Productions.

The air-temperatures of Queensland are high at all seasons. The rainfall is very heavy in the northern parts and especially along the whole coastal belt. In the south-west there is a rapid decrease in the amount which falls. Brisbane has an average rainfall of 50 inches, while in the plains 10° to the west the average fall is often as low as 10 inches, though it sometimes reaches 40 inches.

The cultivated plants of the coastal belt vary from maize and millets in the south to sugar in the centre, and rice, bananas and other tropical products in the north. Oranges, pineapples and grapes grow well in the south. The cooler highlands leading to the Darling Downs produce wheat, and are being developed as dairy-farming districts. Westward, in the drier zone, sheep are reared in large numbers on the Darling Downs and on the western plains. Forests cover much of the well-watered highlands, with 'scrub' land in the west. From the forests, eucalyptus, pine and cedar are obtained; and many valuable ornamental hardwoods are grown in the southern parts of the state.

Gold is mined at Charters Towers, Mt Morgan (near Rockhampton) and Gympie; *copper* and *tin* at Herberton ; and *coal* at Ipswich in the Brisbane valley.

Commerce and Towns.

From *Brisbane*, the capital, a coastal railway with many branches leads northward to *Rockhampton*. From each of these ports there are long lines laid over the Cordilleras to the interior pastoral lands. From *Townsville*, in the north, a line runs through Charters Towers westward to *Cloncurry*, the centre of a rich copper district. *Toowoomba* is the centre of the agricultural part of the Darling Downs.

The chief exports of the state are minerals, meat, hides, skins, tallow, wool and sugar. Brisbane has a population nearly one-fourth of the state's total population of 700,000.

South Australia and Northern Territory.

Position, Size, and Surface.

The state of South Australia extends from the central part of the south coast as far north as parallel 26° S. ; and its western and eastern boundaries are meridians 129° E. and 141° E. Its area is three times that of the British Isles, but only half this area is occupied by settlers. Northern Territory lies to the north of South Australia.

The chief high land is the Flinders range, separating the lake basin from the Murray basin. This range of hills continues southward, separating the Gulf of St Vincent from the lower Murray. To the west of the salt lakes lies a low plateau, the greater part of which is desert.

Climate and Natural Productions.

Air-temperatures increase in a northward direction. Summer rains are only slight ; winter rains are heaviest in the south-east.   The average annual fall is 20 inches at Adelaide.   The interior of the country has a very low rainfall.

The Mediterranean type of climate of the south-east helps to ripen large crops of wheat.   Vines are very productive, over 3,000,000 gallons of wine being produced

Australian Vine in Fruit

in one year.   Mediterranean fruits, such as olives, oranges, lemons, peaches, and apricots, are cultivated, and these along with currants are produced at the Renmark irrigation colony on the north bank of the Murray.   Dairy-farming and sheep-rearing receive considerable attention in the state, but the dry summer does not produce good pasture.   *Copper* is the chief metal produced from mines near Wallaroo.

Commerce and Towns.

A railway leads northward from *Adelaide*, the capital, to *Port Augusta*, the wheat port at the head of Spencer Gulf; and thence northward, through the Lake Basin, to *Oodnadatta*. The Trans-Australian railway connects Port Augusta with Kalgoorlie in Western Australia. The New South Wales silver mines at Willyama are connected by rail with Adelaide, from which town a line runs south-east to the state of Victoria.

Adelaide, the capital, has half the population of the whole state (450,000). Its port is *Port Adelaide* on the shores of the Gulf of St Vincent.

Western Australia.

Position, Size, and Surface.

That portion of the continent which lies west of meridian 129° E. is known as Western Australia. It is over eight times as large as the British Isles, and nearly all of it is a low tableland. Its river courses are numerous, but many of them are scarcely ever occupied by running streams. The coastal plains of the south-west are the important parts. The settlements in the interior have been formed owing to the vast mineral wealth.

Climate and Natural Productions.

The northern triangular portion of the state lies within the Tropics, and receives near the coast heavy rains during the first quarter of the year. The interior of this triangle is dry, and being unable to support the growth of vegetation is a great sandy desert. In the cooler south-west the climate is like that of the Riviera, and the average annual rainfall (chiefly winter rains) is over 20 inches. In this part there are valuable forests from which jarrah and other valuable hardwoods are obtained in large quantities. Wheat is the chief crop in the south-west; and fruits, such as those produced in South Australia, are important. Sheep and cattle rearing are growing industries in the river valleys, and on the coastal slopes of the plateau.

£4,000,000 worth of *gold* is annually produced from the Coolgardie and Murchison goldfields. *Boulder* and *Kalgoorlie* are the chief centres. *Coal* outcrops east of *Bunbury.*

Commerce and Towns.

The railway system extends along the south-west coast to the two goldfields, and to the fine natural harbour of *Albany* in the south. Kalgoorlie is connected by the Trans-Australian line with Port Augusta in South Australia. Gold, timber, wool, pearl and shells (from Shark's Bay) are exported, chiefly through *Fremantle*, the artificial port of the capital *Perth.* Out of a population of 330,000 people, 133,000 reside at the capital and its port.

New Zealand.

Position and Size.

Separated from Australia by a steamer journey of 1200 miles, the islands of New Zealand are even more isolated from the other parts of the 'dry' land of the world than is Australia. The general trend of the islands is S.W.—N.E., with a northern off-shoot at right angles to this direction. The largest of the islands, North, South and Stewart Islands, stretch southward from parallel 34° S. to parallel 47° S., a position similar to that of Tunis, Sicily and Italy in the 'Old World.' The total area of the islands controlled by the Dominion government is less than that of the British Isles.

Mt Cook

Surface and General Features.

From the south-western point of South Island, a mountain range runs diagonally across the island, continuing in North Island near to the east coast and ending in East Cape. This range, known in South Island as the Southern Alps, is higher in South than in North Island. It rises in South Island to Mt Cook, which is 12,000 feet above sea-level. This and many neighbouring peaks are snow-capped, and from their great snow-fields large glaciers descend westward and eastward. On the west they extend down very steep slopes to within 700 ft. of sea-level; and on the east the water produced by the melting of some of the ice and snow feeds many long, narrow lakes. The eastern side of the Southern Alps slopes gently to an alluvial plain, the widest and flattest part of which is known as the Canterbury Plains.

The larger part of North Island runs in a north-westerly direction, and has in its northern peninsular portion a very low average altitude. Almost in the centre of North Island a group of mountains rises to heights varying from 1 mile to 1¾ miles above sea-level. These mountains are volcanic cones, Tongariro bearing several cones one of which emits hot gases and at times fragments of rock. Ruapehu, the highest cone, is snow-clad and has a large hot lake within its crater. Eighty miles or more to the west of this group of slightly active volcanoes, lies another snow-clad volcanic cone—Egmont (8300 ft.). To the north of the central volcanic belt runs the Waikato, New Zealand's longest river, which feeds and drains Lake Taupo, the largest lake of the Dominion. From the northern shores of Taupo to the Bay of Plenty, there is a region of hot springs, geysers, and mud-ejecting volcanoes.

Coasts.

The western coasts of South Island are very rugged, the southern part being a fiord coast. North of the fiord coast good harbours are rare. On the northern coast of North Island, the Hauraki Gulf leads to Auckland harbour. Cook Strait, separating North from South Island, provides an important route to Port Nicholson, the harbour of Wellington, in the south of North Island. The east coast of South Island has two good harbours, each lying north of a peninsula. Banks peninsula shelters Port Lyttelton, and the Otago peninsula the port of Dunedin.

Climate and Natural Productions.

The heating power of the Sun's rays is nowhere at its greatest in New Zealand. A natural decrease in heating power is experienced from north to south. There is considerable modification of air-temperatures, on account of the high altitude of the Southern Alps, and especially because of the nearness of all places to the seas. The chief winds of summer are from a northern quarter, bringing rain, especially on the west coast. In the winter half-year west winds blow—frequently very violently—and the west coast rainfall becomes very heavy. At Hokitika the average annual fall is 116 inches, at Wellington 50 inches, and at Auckland 42 inches.

Nearly a quarter of New Zealand is forested, the chief tree being the kauri pine. Kauri forests are found only north of parallel 39° S., and in the north of the Auckland peninsula. Red, white and black pine and other ornamental woods are also abundant. In the swampy lands around the Waikato valley native flax grows abundantly. The drier plains to the west of Hawke's Bay, in North Island, and to the east of the Southern Alps of South Island form good pasture-ground for the 24 million sheep now reared in the Dominion. The North Island pastures also support large herds of cattle.

Oats, wheat and barley are the chief crops, the Canterbury Province producing wheat, and the cooler Otago Province producing oats. In the east of Auckland

Province, maize is grown, and the equable climate of this province with its dry summer renders it possible to ripen grapes, oranges, lemons, and peaches.

Gold is produced in the Thames district, which lies south of Hauraki Gulf. At Reefton on the western slopes of the Southern Alps, at Ross to the south, and in the Otago rivers, gold is washed from the river deposits, and hill-sides. The total annual output of gold is valued at £2,000,000. *Coal* is found west of the Southern Alps, near Westport and Greymouth. In the northern part of North Island, *kauri-gum* is obtainable by digging on the site of kauri forests. The gum is exported for the manufacture of varnish.

People and administration.

There are nearly 50,000 Polynesians living in New Zealand, known by the name of Maoris. These brown people appear to have migrated from Tahiti and the neighbouring Society Islands, perhaps 1000 years ago. The majority of the Maoris live in Auckland Province, and especially near the geysers.

Tasman, who saw these islands in 1642, did not land ; but in 1779, Captain Cook landed, and later mapped the coasts, naming many of the bays, peninsulas and mountains. In 1840, the British Government annexed the islands, ruling them through governors for fifteen years, until the local parliament was established. The legislative power is now vested in the Governor, and a general assembly of two chambers. In 1907 the Colony received the title of the Dominion of New Zealand. There are now over 1 million people in the Dominion the majority of the people being Protestants.

Commerce and Towns.

From Wellington railways run northward to Auckland, and to the west and east coasts of North Island ; and another line connects Christchurch, the inland centre of the Canterbury Plains, with Invercargill. There is a daily service of steamers from Wellington to Port Lyttelton. Nearly 90 % of the total trade is done

Maori Chief

with the United Kingdom, Australian states, and India. Wool, butter, cheese, 'frozen' meat, gold, hides and skins are the chief exports.   The chief imports are clothing, iron and steel goods, and machinery.

Of the ten towns with a population over 10,000, the chief are *Auckland*, the centre of the timber trade, *Wellington*, the capital, *Christchurch* with its port of Lyttelton, and *Dunedin*.

CHAPTER VIII

NORTH AMERICA

Position and Size.

The continent of North America stretches like a V between parallels 70° N. and 10° N., and it lies in almost equal portions on either side of meridian 100° W. The northern archipelago, including Greenland, stretches to within a few degrees of the North Pole, and the Republic of Panama, in the south, connects North with South America.

The area of this continent is more than twice that of Europe.

Surface and General Features.

The western part of the continent, from north to south, is a mountainous country. Plateaux of varying width, bounded on the west and on the east by high rims of mountains, are also crossed by mountain chains. These mountain chains may be conveniently referred to as a system of Cordilleras. The Cordilleras are widest where crossed by parallel 40° N.; and they are terminated in the south near parallel 18° N. by a west—east range of mountains, carrying volcanic cones. The eastern rim of the plateaux is generally known as the Rocky Mountains, and the western rim as the Alaskan, Cascade, and Sierra Nevada. West of this rim, there is a coast range. In Mexico, the rims are known as the eastern and western Sierra Madre. Many of the peaks in the western rim of the Cordilleras are volcanic cones. The isthmus portion of Central America is crossed by several west—east ridges, bearing volcanic cones.

On the eastern side of the continent, a mountain system, having a S.W.—N.E. direction, extends from 32° N. to the island of Newfoundland. Its eastern part, known as the Appalachian highlands, has long ridges of hilly country separated by deeply-cut valleys. To the west of the Appalachian ridges, the Alleghany plateau slopes very gradually to the north-west, while on the eastern side of the ridges, a somewhat steeper slope leads to a coastal plain, which is widest near parallel 30° N.

Between the Cordilleras and the Appalachians there lies a vast plain. North of 50° N., this land slopes gently to Hudson Bay, and to the south the plains slope to the deep Gulf of Mexico.

Rivers and Lakes.

From the plateaux of the Cordilleras, four large rivers drain westward to the Pacific Ocean. In the far north, the Yukon reaches the ocean without crossing the plateau rim ; but the Fraser, Columbia, and Colorado have cut deep gaps into the western rim, and the Columbia has in addition cut a gap through the parallel, but quite distinct, coast range. The Sacramento, flowing south between the Sierra Nevada and the coast range, empties to the Pacific Ocean through a gap—the Golden Gate—in the latter range. In the widest part of the high plateau of the Cordilleras, there is a 'Great Basin' of inland drainage, containing Great Salt Lake.

From the eastern side of the Cordilleras, many rivers drain down steep slopes to the low central plains of the continent. The Athabasca and Peace rivers, feeding Lake Athabasca, drain north to the larger Great Slave Lake, the outflow of which, known as the Mackenzie, runs north-west to the Arctic Ocean, receiving on its way the waters of Great Bear Lake. Further south, the North and South Saskatchewan rivers flow eastward. From the south, the Saskatchewan receives the waters of Lake

Winnipeg, which is fed by the northward flowing Red river and by the overflow of Lakes Manitoba and Winnipegosis. The river leading from these lakes to Hudson Bay is known as the Nelson. The southern part of the central plain is drained by the Mississippi, which winds about meridian 90° W., receiving many long tributaries from both the Cordilleras and the Alleghany plateau. The Missouri and others feed the main stream from the west, and the Ohio (with its tributary the Tennessee) carries westward the waters of the Alleghany plateau. From the junction of the Missouri and Mississippi, the river flows through a widening plain, and south of parallel 30° S. the river is forming a large delta. South-west of the Mississippi basin, the Rio Grande runs south and east to the Gulf of Mexico.

From the Appalachians relatively short and swift rivers flow eastward to the Atlantic Ocean. From north to south these are: St John, Connecticut, Hudson, Delaware, Susquehanna, Potomac and James.

Between the Hudson Bay rivers and the Mississippi basin, there lies the largest sheet of fresh water on the Earth's surface. Five great lakes—Superior, Michigan, Huron, Erie, Ontario—empty ·into the St Lawrence, which flows north-east to the Gulf of St Lawrence. Various rapids and falls interrupt the drainage from one lake to another (except in the case of Michigan and Huron), the most noteworthy being the Niagara Falls, 167 ft. in depth, between Lakes Erie and Ontario. The Ottawa runs west, south, and finally east to the St Lawrence, and a few miles further down-stream, the Richelieu empties the waters of Lake Champlain northward to the main stream.

Coasts.

The north coast of this great peninsula, and the coasts of the neighbouring Arctic archipelago are rocky and indented. For a great part of the year these coasts are surrounded by ice—the frozen surface of the seas.

Hudson Strait leading to Hudson Bay is ice-free for only one-third of the year; and the Davis and other straits further north are ice-free for even shorter periods. As the glaciers fed by the great ice-sheet of Greenland push out to sea they form icebergs. These icebergs are carried southward in spring and early summer to the fiord coasts of Labrador and Newfoundland, there becoming stranded. In exceptional seasons the icebergs drift much further south, and vessels sailing between the Atlantic coasts of North America and Europe have to steer a southerly course during the summer half-year in order to avoid these dangerous wanderers.

Iceberg off Greenland

The island of Newfoundland is separated from the Labrador peninsula by the Strait of Belle Isle, and from Cape Breton Island by Cabot Strait. In the Gulf of St Lawrence lie Anticosti and Prince Edward Island; and its mouth is partly protected from icebergs by Newfoundland and Cape Breton Island. The latter island, like its continuation the Nova Scotia peninsula, has rocky and indented coasts washed by the Atlantic. The Bay of Fundy and its two northern bays reach far inland, and nearly sever Nova Scotia from the mainland. The east coast of North America from the head of Fundy

Bay to the mouth of the Hudson is a rocky coast, with many 'drowned' valleys ; but the coast southward to the Gulf of Mexico is shallow, and sandy reefs lie off-shore. The low Florida peninsula is separated from the coralline limestone Bahama Islands and from the mountainous West Indies by Florida Strait. The Strait of Yucatan separates a similar low peninsula from these islands. The Caribbean Sea lies between the eastern side of the isthmian portion of America and the south-western sides of the West Indies.

The western coasts of the continent are everywhere rocky. The coast range, represented by the California peninsula in the south and by the many islands off the coasts of British Columbia and Alaska, has only one good opening in the United States—the Golden Gate. The much indented mainland of British Columbia is very similar to the west coast of Norway. In the far north, the Alaska peninsula leads to the Aleutian Islands of Asia ; while near the Arctic Circle, Bering Strait not 40 miles wide separates the New from the Old World.

Climate.

(a) **Air-temperatures.**

The mainland of North America stretches through the same latitudes as Europe and North Africa. The western part of the 'Old World' widens in a southward direction, whereas North America becomes narrower. The tropical territories of this continent are almost insignificant when compared with those of the 'Old World' ; and the wide, northern part of America is far greater than the similar lands of North Europe. Consequently, in June, when the Sun's noon rays are shining vertically near to and south of the Tropic of Cancer, America has far less land surface heated by these rays than has the eastern land of Africa. The high air-temperatures produced are not so widely spread in the 'New World.' In December, when the Sun's heating

power is at its lowest and the Earth's surface is cooling
in the northern hemisphere, much lower temperatures
are produced here than in Europe.   More than half the
area of North America has in January an average air-
temperature below 32° F.

(b)   Rainfall.

The isthmus and the Atlantic side of the northern
lands are in summer swept by winds, whose movement
tends to make them saturated with water-vapour.
Rain falls therefore in these districts, and the amount
diminishes from the Atlantic coast in a north-westerly
direction.   West of meridian 100° W. the rainfall is low.
The western parts of the peninsula do not receive much
summer rain.

In the winter half-year, western North America
comes under the influence of rain-shedding winds, the
fall decreasing eastward and southward.   The wide
plateaux of the Cordilleras have little rainfall, being
shielded by the western mountain rims from west
winds.

Plants and Animals.

In the north tundra conditions prevail.   The gradual
increase of air-temperatures southward, together with
the increase in rainfall, develops the coniferous shrubs
into dense forests of coniferous trees.   This coniferous
zone extends from the Atlantic to the Pacific coasts,
except where the low air-temperatures of the Cordilleras
dwarf the trees until tundra conditions again appear.
The chief trees of this coniferous forest are the black
and white spruce, and the larch.   South of the Saskatchewan valley, the rainfall is not sufficient in conjunction
with the increasing heat to allow trees to grow.   Thus
the lands east of the Cordilleras, west of meridian 100° W.
and south of the Saskatchewan, are steppes or grass
regions.   Except in this belt of steppes, the conifers
gradually become mixed with deciduous trees leading

southward to evergreen trees. The Cordilleras on their western slopes are covered with conifers, the dividing line between coniferous and warmer types of vegetation rising higher southward, till within the Tropics at a height of 10,000 ft. there are dense forests of spruce and fir. The low parts of the tropical lands bear abundant tropical vegetation, which gives place in the higher parts of the hill-slopes to evergreen, deciduous, coniferous and finally treeless zones.

In the tundra musk oxen, caribou and polar bears roam. To the south, the forest zone shelters a variety of fur-bearing animals, including beaver, brown bear, marten and fox; while the grass regions—once the feeding grounds of large herds of bison—now have few wild animals other than deer. Mexico and the southern countries of the isthmus have large quadrupeds, such as the tapir, jaguar and puma. The warmer waters of the south are infested by alligators and crocodiles.

In the cold, swift rivers of British Columbia, Washington, Oregon, and elsewhere, salmon and many other fresh-water fish abound. Cod, herring, and various white-fish are caught over the shallow banks of Newfoundland, east of the Gulf of St Lawrence, and over the shallows further south.

Agriculture and Pasture.

The steppes of the interior are the great pastoral regions of the continent, supporting large herds of cattle.

From the Saskatchewan valleys to the latitude of the south end of the great lakes, wheat is the chief crop. North of the latitude of the Mississippi-Ohio junction and south of the great lakes, maize (indian corn) is the chief cereal. South of the maize belt cotton is important, with tobacco in the northern half and rice in the southern half of the cotton belt.

The mild and rainy climate of Nova Scotia and Prince Edward Island is favourable for the cultivation of apples. The Ontario peninsula has air-temperatures

Cod-fishing fleet, St John's, Newfoundland

similar to those of France, and receives abundant rainfall. It produces apples, pears, peaches, plums and grapes. Parts of British Columbia are famous for apples and other fruits. The California valley, lying between the coast range and the Sierra Nevada, has a Mediterranean type of climate. Peaches, pears, plums, prunes, grapes, oranges and lemons are typical products of this valley.

In the tropical lands, coffee and cacao, bananas and oranges, cotton and tobacco are characteristic agricultural products. In the higher plateaux of Mexico wheat is an important crop. Cattle, goats and sheep are pastured in the grass regions of the drier parts of these plateaux.

Minerals.

Gold is produced in the upper Yukon valley, and in the Sierra Nevada ; *silver* in the plateau north of the St Lawrence, and in Mexico ; *copper* and *iron* around the head of the great lakes ; *coal* in Cape Breton and Vancouver Islands, in the Rocky Mountains, and especially in the Alleghany plateau ; and *petroleum* is extensively pumped from the north part of the Alleghany plateau, and in California.

British North America.

Position and Size.

British North America—the Dominion of Canada and Newfoundland—stretches from the Atlantic to the Pacific coasts. It is separated from the United States territory of Alaska by meridian 141° W. ; and from the United States of America by an irregular boundary 3000 miles long. From the west coast to meridian 95° W., the boundary follows parallel 49° N. After reaching the Lake of the Woods, the boundary runs south-east through Lakes Superior, Huron, Erie and Ontario, and along the St Lawrence as far as parallel 45° N. This parallel is followed for some distance, after which the boundary runs north-east to the St John river, and by another meridian to the River St Croix.

British North America is larger in size than the continent of Europe, Canada being 30 times the size of the British Isles, and Newfoundland (with Labrador) a little larger than our islands.

Surface and General Features.

South of the Gulf of St Lawrence lie the Appalachian ridges of Newfoundland, Cape Breton and Prince Edward islands, Nova Scotia, New Brunswick, and southern Quebec. North of the St Lawrence there is a wide, low plateau from which rivers descend in steps to the St Lawrence on the south and to Hudson Bay in the north. When the rivers approach the Laurentian edge of the plateau, they are broken by falls. The chief of these rivers is the Ottawa.

The peninsula between Lakes Huron, Erie and Ontario is the most southerly portion of Canada. Lake Superior is drained by the Ste Marie river to Huron. The St Clair and Detroit rivers carry Huron's waters to Lake Erie. The Niagara river, broken by Niagara Falls and rapids, leads the waters of Lake Erie into Lake Ontario the overflow of the latter lake being received by the St Lawrence.

From the low-lying country bordered by the Arctic Ocean and Hudson Bay, the land gradually rises to the Cordilleras in the west. The Athabasca—Mackenzie leads the surface waters northward across this plain to the Arctic Ocean. The Saskatchewan—Nelson drains eastward to Hudson Bay. Each river receives tributaries from great lakes, of which Lake Winnipeg fed by the northward flowing Red river is the most important.

The Cordilleras separating these plains from the Pacific seaboard are narrow. They include many mountain ranges, trending N.W.—S.E., with deep valleys between them. From east going west, these ranges are known as the Rocky, Selkirk, Gold and (near the coast) Cascade ranges. The many islands off the Pacific coast represent the partly submerged coast range. The Cordilleras are drained by two great rivers, the Columbia and Fraser.

Ice-Pack, Strait of Belle Isle

Coasts.

The north and north-east coasts of British North America are rocky and indented in places: but they are ice-bound for a great part of the year. Hudson Strait, leading into the shallow Hudson Bay, is the most important opening. From this strait southward, the Atlantic coast is much indented. The Strait of Belle Isle is often a mass of floating icebergs, but Cabot

Strait is sheltered somewhat by the eastward protruding coast of Newfoundland. The harbour of Halifax, N.S., is very large and ice-free all the year round ; while the seas washing the rocky coasts of the Gulf of St Lawrence are frozen during the winter months. Anticosti, in this gulf, is a forested island with no good harbour ; but Prince Edward Island, lying in the south part of this great bay, is very indented. The Bay of Fundy, which separates the west shore of Nova Scotia from the east shore of New Brunswick, is noted for its high tides. The harbour at the mouth of the St John river, on the western shores of Fundy Bay, is (like the harbour of Halifax) open all the year round.

The west coast of British North America, which extends only from parallel 49° N. to parallel 55° N., presents fine scenery to the tourist, and resembles the west coasts of Ireland and Scotland in its indented coasts and island fringes. Vancouver and Queen Charlotte Islands are the largest of these.

Climate.

The greater part of British North America lies in latitudes the same as those of the British Isles. The great lakes, St Lawrence valley, and the Atlantic peninsular and insular portions lie south of our latitudes ; and the district drained by the Yukon and Mackenzie rivers lies in the latitudes of Norway. It follows therefore that British Columbia, Alberta, Saskatchewan, Manitoba, and the northern parts of Ontario, Quebec, and Labrador receive the same amount of heat from the Sun as do corresponding parts of our islands. The Lakes, the St Lawrence valley and the Atlantic provinces all receive greater heat, and the northern districts less heat. The lake peninsula, lying in the latitudes of south France and north Spain, has the highest air-temperatures ; and the high peaks of the Cordilleras have the lowest air-temperatures.

In summer the prevailing direction of the winds is from the east. Consequently the Atlantic provinces have modified air-temperatures, and much rain, during their summer months. The cooling effect and the amount of the rainfall decrease westward, until in the hilly country east of the Cordilleras summers are hot and dry. The Pacific slopes of the Cordilleras do not receive much rain in summer. In the winter half-year the prevailing winds blow from the west, bringing to the Pacific lands warm air and making their climate very mild. Rain also falls in great amount. Eastern Canada is, in these months, swept by cold air from the north-west plains, and consequently has very low air-temperatures. All river- and lake-surfaces freeze, and snow falls heavily.

Plants and Animals.

North of the 50° F. July isotherm, the tundra type of vegetation is characteristic. Southward small shrubs lead to the extensive coniferous forests, which stretch from sea to sea except in the highest parts of the Cordilleras. In the provinces east of meridian 100 ° W., this forest belt comes south beyond the St Lawrence ; but west of that meridian and south of the Saskatchewan the rainfall is not sufficient to allow trees to grow in large numbers. The Cordilleras are tree-clad to high altitudes, but their valleys are in places treeless. Spruce, fir, hemlock, pine, laurel, poplar and maple are the chief trees.

In the forest zones, wild animals are still abundant. Fur-bearing animals are hunted by Indians for their skins. The plains to the south support antelope and deer. The forest-clad slopes of the western mountains shelter caribou, deer, bear (grizzly and black) and other 'game.'

The 'Great Bank of Newfoundland' is the feeding-ground of cod, mackerel, herring and haddock. Lobsters and oysters are plentiful in the seas of Nova Scotia and Prince Edward Island. The rivers of British Columbia swarm with salmon and trout ; and these and many other fish are to be found in the lakes and rivers of the interior.

Agriculture.

In the basins of the Red and Saskatchewan rivers wheat is grown on a very large scale. Oats are cultivated more than wheat in the colder east. The

Field of oats, Manitoba

warm lake peninsula of Ontario is covered with fruit farms—apples, peaches, pears, plums, and grapes being grown successfully. The warm south-west parts of Nova Scotia and Prince Edward Island are renowned apple-growing districts. British Columbia produces apples, pears, plums and cherries.

The chief pastoral districts of Canada lie east of the Cordilleras. The 'ranches' of South Alberta support large numbers of cattle, horses and sheep. In the most easterly provinces dairy-farming is increasing in importance.

Minerals.

Coal is the most valuable of Canada's minerals. Coalfields are being developed in Cape Breton Island ; in the upper Saskatchewan valley ; on the slopes of the Rocky Mountains; and in the south of Vancouver Island. *Gold* is mined in the Cordilleras of British Columbia and Yukon. *Silver* mines are of great importance at Cobalt, in the upper Ottawa valley ; *copper, iron,* and other minerals are also worked. Newfoundland has valuable *iron* and *copper* ores.

People, Race, and Religion.

The latest census returns for Canada show that the population now numbers over 7,206,643. During the ten years 1901—1911, the increase has been over 34 %. The greatest increase was in Alberta and Saskatchewan, where there were the large increases of 413 % and 439 % respectively. In the Yukon, there has been a decrease of over 68 %, and in the North-West Territories a decrease of 15 %. There are nearly 2 people to every square mile in the whole country, with 42 in Prince Edward Isle, 23 in Nova Scotia, over 12 in New Brunswick, 9 in Ontario, nearly 6 in Manitoba and Quebec, and less than 2 in Saskatchewan, Alberta, and British Columbia. In the Yukon and North-West Territories, there is only one person to every 80 square miles.

A large number of the people living in the St Lawrence valley speak French, and are Roman Catholic in religion. In the western provinces Protestants are more numerous, and there are also in the west considerable numbers of Germans, Russians, and Scandinavians. British Columbia has a fair number of Asiatic immigrants, chiefly Chinese. The native and Eskimo races number less than 2 % of the population. There are several Indian reserves in the Dominion, especially in the western plains. In the forests of the north, many

14—2

Indians live by trapping the fur-bearing animals and selling the skins to British traders.

In the colony of Newfoundland and Labrador, there are a quarter of a million people, a third of whom are Roman Catholics.

Industries and Communications.

Agriculture, stock-raising, mining, fisheries, lumbering and the fur trade, are the chief occupations in British North America. In south Ontario there are many large engineering works. The waterfalls of the Ste Marie, Niagara, Ottawa,. and other rivers are being utilised for the generation of electric power, and near each of these districts large engineering works are springing up. Saw mills are important near the Ottawa falls.

The waterways of Eastern Canada are useless for a third of the year, while in places they are much impeded by rapids. The various canals and locks between the great lakes have developed the river traffic of Canada to a great extent, and through them grain is carried from the twin ports of Fort William—Port Arthur, on Lake Superior, to the great river port of Montreal. There the grain is transferred to ocean steamers.

The railway systems of Canada have been, and are likely to continue, important means of developing the western plains. The chief railway systems are: Canadian Pacific, Grand Trunk, Grand Trunk Pacific and Canadian Northern.

Commerce and Ports.

The total trade of Canada has an annual value of over £400,000,000. The chief exports of the Dominion are wheat and flour, timber, cheese, bacon, cattle, silver and copper ores and iron; and the chief imports are manufactured goods such as iron and steel, woollen and cotton goods.

There is a large internal trade; and the railway

The St Lawrence at Montreal

companies working in the western plains have built a large number of grain elevators alongside their railroads, in which to store wheat *en route* for the lake ports, *Port Arthur* and *Fort William.* *Montreal,* at the head of the St Lawrence navigation for ocean vessels, is the great summer port of the Dominion. *St John,* N.B., and *Halifax,* N.S., are the winter ports. *Vancouver* is the starting point of vessels trading with Japan, Australia and New Zealand.

St John's is the chief port and town of Newfoundland.

Administration, Divisions, and Towns.

The Dominion of Canada consists of nine provinces (Nova Scotia, Prince Edward Island, New Brunswick, Quebec, Ontario, Manitoba, Saskatchewan, Alberta, and British Columbia), and several territories. *Ottawa* is the seat of the Federal Government, which consists of a Governor-General (representing the King), a Senate and a House of Commons. Each province has its lieutenant-governor, parliament, and administration. Newfoundland is independent of the Dominion and has its own Governor and Parliament.

Montreal, the largest port of Canada, has nearly 500,000 inhabitants. *Toronto* is a banking and manufacturing centre on the northern shore of Lake Ontario. *Winnipeg,* in the centre of the wheat belt, is situated on the Red river. *Vancouver* is the port of the Pacific. *Ottawa* is the capital of the Dominion, and is a lumbering centre. *Hamilton,* the western port of Lake Ontario, is a manufacturing city. *Quebec* has wood-pulp factories. *Halifax* and *St John* are the chief towns of the maritime provinces. *Calgary, Regina,* and *Edmonton* are rising towns in the western plains. *Victoria,* on the island of Vancouver, is the capital of British Columbia.

The United States of America.

Position and Size.

From Pacific to Atlantic, and from the Canadian border on the north to the Rio Grande and the Gulf of Mexico on the south, 48 States, known as the United States of America, together occupy an area of 3½ million square miles—nearly 30 times the area of the British Isles.

Geyser in Yellowstone Park

Surface and General Features.

Three belts of country may be distinguished in this great area—the Cordilleras in the west, the Appalachian system in the east, and the plains between the two mountain systems. The Cordilleras, from west to east, consists of a coast range, a long north—south valley, the Cascade and Sierra Nevada ranges, a high plateau (nearly 1,000 miles wide along parallel 40° N.), and the Rocky Mountains in the east. In the northern part of the Rocky Mountains the Yellowstone National Park is a region of mud-ejecting volcanoes, geysers, and deeply-cut valleys. The western rim of the plateau also has extinct volcanoes and magnificent scenery.

In the east, the Appalachian system runs S.W.—N.E., coming near to the Atlantic in its northern part. It is highest in the north and south, and low in its central portion. To the west of this belt of ridges and valleys, the Alleghany plateau slopes to the great plains. These plains are connected with the Atlantic coast plain by a low plain round the southern end of the Appalachians. The Florida peninsula is a low, limestone plain, pitted with innumerable lakes.

Rivers and Lakes.

From the Appalachian ranges, rivers run for some distance parallel to the main ridges, and, breaking through these ridges, they drain eastward to the Atlantic. The Hudson is the chief of these, and others are the Connecticut, Delaware, Susquehanna, and Potomac. The western slopes of the Alleghany plateau and the eastern slopes of the Rocky Mountains are drained by rivers to a central waterway, the Mississippi. This river, rising at no great altitude in some small lakes 100 miles west of Lake Superior, runs southward to the Gulf of Mexico, and after passing the Falls of St Anthony at parallel 45° N. it is navigable to its mouth at parallel 30° N. Large quantities of suspended matter are carried into it by the Missouri from the west and by the Ohio from the east. The floods produced by these and other rivers are kept within bounds by means of embankments. Its great delta increases in size after every flood, and the channels in this delta radiate north, east, and south into the Gulf of Mexico.

Lake Michigan is wholly within United States territory. The peninsula between Lakes Erie and Ontario, the St Lawrence river, and the Atlantic is covered by thousands of small lakes. Champlain—which feeds the St Lawrence—is the largest of these. In the plateau of the Cordilleras, Great Salt Lake is a region of inland drainage.

From the Cordilleras the Columbia, Sacramento, and Colorado run to the Pacific Ocean. The Columbia has cut deep gaps through the Cascade and coast ranges. The Sacramento occupies a great part of the California valley, between the coast range and the Sierra Nevada, and drains into San Francisco Bay. The Colorado valley has a wonderful series of cañons, or gorges, in its middle portion.

Coasts.

From parallel 45° N. to the mouth of the Hudson the coast is indented, providing many good harbours. Manhattan Island lies at the mouth of the Hudson river, Staten Island to the south, and Long Island to the east. The southern part of the Atlantic coast is sandy and fringed in places by sand-reefs, swamps, and lagoons. Off the east of the Florida coast there are reefs of coralline limestone. The coasts of the Gulf of Mexico resemble the south part of the Atlantic coast.

The west coast, bordered by the coast range, is broken in two places by the Sacramento and Columbia rivers. In the north Juan da Fuca Strait, between Vancouver Island and Washington State, leads to Puget Sound, a drowned portion of the valley between the coast range and the Cordilleras.

Climate.

Lying south of the latitudes of the British Isles and north of the Tropic of Cancer, all places in the United

States receive more heat from the Sun's rays than we
do, but only the extreme south of California peninsula
receives the vertical noon rays of the Sun. A general
increase in air-temperatures is natural from north to
south, but in the high lands of the Cordilleras and Appalachians the air-temperatures recorded are not so high
as those of the low-lying states in the same latitudes.

The summer winds bring rain to the south-east parts
of this country. The rainfall generally decreases inland.
The plains west of the Mississippi do not receive much
rain, though summer is generally the rainy season. In
winter the western states are well watered. The high
western rims of the high plateaux help to saturate the
air and increase the amount of rainfall, especially in
the California valley ; but they make the interior
plateaux almost rainless.

Plants and Animals.

The well-watered eastern part of this country is
wooded. In the northern parts coniferous trees, such
as spruce, are still abundant, while southward deciduous
and evergreen trees replace the colder types. The
south parts of the eastern states have cypress and cedar
forests. The seaward slopes of the Cascade and Sierra
Nevada ranges are covered by dense forests of conifers.
West of the Mississippi grasses flourish, becoming of a
parched type in the slopes at the foot of the Rocky
Mountains. The dry plateaux are covered by drought-
resisting plants.

The bear, elk, deer, mountain sheep, and goat are
fast disappearing, except in the specially reserved areas.
There are still many snakes, alligators, and crocodiles in
the warm south.

Agriculture and Pasture.

From the international boundary to the latitude of
the south end of the great lakes, wheat is the chief
crop. South of the wheat zone maize is the chief crop,

wheat being produced in smaller quantities. The output of maize is nearly four times as great as that of wheat. Much of this crop is used for the feeding of millions of hogs. The states around the lower Missouri and Ohio rivers are the chief maize-growing districts. Further to the south, the hot, wet summer in the low-lying lands favours the cultivation of rice and sugar, produced chiefly in Louisiana and Texas. The states lying south of the latitude of the Mississippi—Ohio confluence are important producers of cotton, the acreage of this crop increasing generally in a southward direction. Texas and Georgia are the chief cotton-growing states. Tobacco is grown chiefly in Kentucky, North Carolina, Virginia, and Tennessee. Sugar, oranges and pineapples are important products of the Gulf states.

In the north part of the Pacific states wheat is produced, and the California valley is becoming a great fruit-growing district. Oranges and lemons are exported from south California ; grapes are grown and wine is produced in large quantities in the north. Peaches, pears, plums, and prunes are other important products.

The dry regions east of the Rocky Mountains and west of meridian 100° W. are the great stock-raising lands. Several of the eastern states are dairy-farming districts, New York state being the chief.

Fisheries.

Off the north part of the Atlantic coast there are valuable cod, haddock, halibut, mackerel, and herring fisheries, and in the shallow Chesapeake Bay oysters are farmed. The fresh-water fisheries are also important both in the east and west. The Columbia river is extremely rich in salmon ; California also has salmon fisheries.

Minerals.

The state of Pennsylvania is the great producer of *anthracite*, and also produces one-third of the United States' output of ordinary *coal*. Parts of its coalfield extend into Ohio and West Virginia. The Illinois coalfield comes next in order of importance. The coalfields in the Alleghany plateau and in Illinois are also *petroleum* fields. California produces over one-third of the republic's output of petroleum. *Iron* ores are plentiful around the north-western and southern shores of Lake Superior. The iron-ore is transported over the lakes to Cleveland, Erie, and other ports on the south shores of Lake Erie. Some of the ore is smelted at these ports, and some is taken by train to Pittsburg, in the Ohio valley, the centre of the Pennsylvania coalfield. *Copper* and *gold*, and smaller values of *lead, silver*, and *zinc* are also produced.

People and Religion.

Although the area of the United States is less than that of Canada, its population is more than twelve times as great as that of the neighbouring Dominion. 300,000 Indians now remain of the native races, many of them living in specially reserved districts. The negro population numbers 10 millions. Georgia, Mississippi, South Carolina, and Alabama have a large negro population.

The white population of the States numbered a century ago 6 millions, while in 1920 there were over 105 million people.

Protestant bodies are the most numerous of the religious denominations. There are 16 million Roman Catholics. The States have nearly 600 universities and colleges, 1½ million pupils in secondary schools, and 20 millions in elementary schools.

Industries.

The industries connected with the preparation of food are the most valuable of the many industries of the States. Meat-packing is the chief of these, especially at Chicago and Cincinnati. Flour-milling is the staple industry at St Paul and Minneapolis, near the St Anthony Falls of the Mississippi. Lumbering, south and east of the Lakes, is also noteworthy. The textile industries are well developed in the New England states. Here the humid atmosphere, abundant water-power, and the nearness of the cotton fields of the southern Atlantic states all help to develop these industries. Much of the United States' cotton crop is consumed in the country; the value of the cotton goods exported being over ⅓ of that of the raw cotton exported. Rhode Island and Massachusetts manufacture large amounts of cotton and woollen goods, and the latter state is also a centre for the boot and shoe industries. New York state has an enormous output of clothing. The iron and steel industries are next in value. Pennsylvania is the chief state engaged in the iron and steel trade. The neighbouring states have also many engine-shops and railway-car works.

Communications.

The great lakes provide exceptional facilities for communication by water ; and, in conjunction with the Erie Canal, trade may be carried on with the Hudson. No less important as a navigable waterway is the Mississippi and its tributary, the Ohio.

There are over 250,000 miles of railway in the United States. From New York lines run north-east, north, north-west, west, and south-west. Chicago is the converging point of all the railways which serve the wheat-producing districts lying west of the lakes, and San Francisco is the great Pacific terminus of several important trans-continental lines.

Commerce and Ports.

The total annual trade of the United States is over £2,000,000,000. The United Kingdom is the States' best customer, receiving about ½ her goods, and sending to the republic ½ the goods which she requires. Manufactured goods, raw materials, and food-stuffs are the chief articles of trade—the export values in each class being greater than the import values. Iron and steel goods, meat and dairy products, bread-stuffs and raw cotton are the chief exports. The chief imports are sugar, wool and woollen goods, raw silk, rubber and chemicals.

Of the British trade with the United States, raw cotton is the most valuable item, and wheat, wheat-flour, maize, bacon, lard, leather, petroleum, tobacco, and cattle are other valuable imports. Linen, cotton, iron, and woollen goods are the chief articles received by the United States from our islands.

New York is the chief port of the country ; the other large ports being *Philadelphia, New Orleans*, the *Puget Sound* ports, *Boston, Baltimore*, and *San Francisco*. The Lake ports do a large amount of local trade, especially in iron-ore and grain.

Administration and Towns.

The original 13 states of the Union have increased to 48. Each state has a governor and two houses of legislature, and sends senators to the Federal Parliament at *Washington*. This parliament consists of the Senate and the House of Representatives. The form of government is republican, the President holding office for four years.

There are 31 cities with a population of over 200,000, and over 100 cities with a population of over 50,000. *New York*, with five million inhabitants, is the chief city. Originally built on Manhattan Island, it now spreads over the west end of Long Island under the name of *Brooklyn*. *Chicago* is a railway, cattle, and grain centre. *Philadelphia* has engineering and textile industries. *St Louis* is a railway and meat-packing centre. *Boston* is the port of the New England states, and *Baltimore* a smaller port on Chesapeake Bay. *Cleveland* is the lake port of *Pittsburg*, and each has iron-smelting industries. *Detroit, Buffalo*, and *Milwaukee* are other noteworthy lake ports, with trade in grain. *Minneapolis* and *St Paul* are milling centres.

New York

From *San Francisco* there are regular sailings to Japan and Australia. *Seattle* is the port of Puget Sound, and *Portland* (Oregon) the port of the Columbia valley. *New Orleans, Galveston,* and *Mobile,* on the shores of the Gulf of Mexico, export cotton.

Central America.

Position and Size.

South of the Rio Grande, and north of parallel 8° N., the mainland of America tapers to the very narrow isthmus of Panama. It is fringed on the east by an archipelago—the West Indies, stretching from the Florida peninsula to the mouth of the river Orinoco, in South America.

This territory is bounded on the west by the Pacific Ocean, and on the east by the Gulf of Mexico and the Caribbean Sea. Central America is over 15 times as large as the British Isles. Mexico is over 5 times the size, while Guatemala, Honduras, Nicaragua, and Cuba each has an area one-third the size of our isles.

Surface and General Features.

Mexico is a high plateau, with higher rims west and east. In the latitude of the south end of the Gulf of Mexico this plateau rises to a high ridge, bearing volcanic cones, of which Orizaba and Popocatapetl are the chief. South of this volcanic ridge there are several other west—east ridges, with low saddles between them. The largest islands of the West Indies reproduce this west—east direction, and have mountain ranges with the same direction.

The interior of Mexico is crossed by many valleys, but rivers only occupy them during rainy seasons. There are several large salt lakes north of the volcanic ridge. The southern part of Nicaragua has an extensive lake (131 ft. above sea-level) which drains to the Caribbean Sea through the river San Juan. East of meridian 80° W. the mountains of Panama are broken by a saddle, the highest part of which is not 300 ft. above sea-level.

The Bahama Islands are composed of coralline limestone. Many of the smaller islands of the West Indies are of volcanic origin. Trinidad is a low, rectangular island off the mainland of South America.

Climate.

In June central Mexico receives the Sun's vertical rays. The great heat thus developed, both in the mainland and in the islands, is tempered by altitude and by sea-breezes. The mountain slopes from about ½ mile to 1½ miles above sea-level have air-temperatures similar to those of the United States south of the lakes; above 1½ miles air-temperatures are like those of the north of the United States and the south of Canada. The highest peaks are snow-clad.

Rain falls abundantly during the hot summer months, the lowest parts of these countries becoming very unhealthy for Europeans during the rainy season.

Natural Productions.

In the low parts of Central America and up the mountain slopes to about ½ mile in altitude there is a luxuriant tropical vegetation, producing mahogany, logwood, rosewood, coco-nut, bananas, and cacao. In the zone up to about 1½ miles in altitude coffee, sugar, maize, and oranges are cultivated. The highest parts have oak and pine forests, and clearings in which wheat is grown and cattle pastured. Coffee is the chief product of Guatemala, Salvador, Nicaragua, and Haiti. Cacao is becoming an important crop, especially in Trinidad. Bananas are grown in Honduras, Costa Rica, and Jamaica, largely for export. Tobacco is the chief crop in Cuba. Since the outbreak of war in Europe in 1914, the cane-sugar crop of Central America has become

very important. Cuba alone produces a third of the
world's cane-sugar crop, and Porto Rico a tenth of Cuba's
crop. The British West Indies and Santo Domingo rank
next as sugar producers.

Sacking coffee, Costa Rica

All the mountain ranges of the mainland are rich
in minerals. *Gold, silver, copper, lead,* and *iron* are
worked, silver being the chief and gold the second
mineral product of Mexico. Trinidad has almost inex-
haustible supplies of *asphalt.*

People and Administration.

There are over 28 million people in Central America,
15 millions being in Mexico, about 2 millions in Cuba,
Haiti, Guatemala, and the British West Indies, and
1 million in Salvador and Porto Rico. On the mainland
Indians are still numerous. There is a large number of

Spaniards, especially in Mexico. The islands have large negro populations.

The Bahamas were perhaps the land-fall of Columbus, when he was seeking a westward passage to the Indies. His discoveries were followed up by Spanish invasion a quarter of a century later, Cortes conquering Mexico and calling it the province of New Spain. The neighbouring insular and isthmian lands also came under Spanish rule. The greater part of Central America is now independent. The mainland is ruled by 7 republics, but a small strip of coastal land— British Honduras—is part of the British Empire. Cuba, Haiti, and Santo Domingo are independent republics, Porto Rico is a United States' territory, and the greater number of the other islands are British.

Industries, Commerce, and Towns.

Mexico has a number of cotton and tobacco factories. The factories of Cuba turn out over 150,000,000 cigars annually. Sugar-mills are at work in several of the republics.

Communication is difficult in most parts of Central America. Roads are bad, and there are practically no navigable waterways. The Mexican plateau is crossed by several railways from the United States; the *City of Mexico* is connected by rail with Vera Cruz; and the low saddles of Tehuantepec and Panama are crossed by railways. The Tehuantepec line joins Salina Cruz on the Pacific to Puerto Mexico on the Gulf. The Panama line from Colon to Panama runs parallel to the Panama Canal.

Silver, gold, coffee, ornamental and dye woods, cacao, sugar, and fruits (bananas, pineapples, and limes) form the chief exports. Cotton goods and machinery are the chief imports.

Havana is the chief port of Cuba, *Tampico, Vera Cruz,* and *Acapulco* the ports of Mexico, *Kingston* the port and capital of Jamaica, and *Belize* the chief seaport of the isthmus.

CHAPTER IX

SOUTH AMERICA

Position and Size.

The peninsular continent of South America lies east of meridian 80° W., and is almost intersected by meridian 60° W. Its northerly point is 12½° N. of the Equator, and its southerly point is 56° S. of the Equator. North and east of the continent lies the Atlantic Ocean, and to the west lies the Pacific Ocean. On the north-west a narrow land boundary separates South America from the Panama Republic. South America is almost twice as large as Europe. Four-fifths of it lies within the Tropics.

Surface and General Features.

The western Cordilleras, or Andes as the whole range is called, have determined the scythe-like shape of the west coast. From the southern part of the continent, the Cordilleras run northward to parallel 18° S., there taking a semi-circular course, and ending as a west—east range along the Caribbean coast. The plateaux of the Andes are widest near the bend of the Cordilleras, and are highest near the Equator. In the wide Bolivian plateau there are several lakes receiving the inland drainage ; Titicaca is the chief of these. Aconcagua (23,080 ft.) is the highest peak of the Andes, and there are several high peaks in the rim east of the widest part of the plateau. The equatorial part of the Cordilleras has volcanic cones, the chief being Chimborazo and Cotopaxi, which are snow-clad, and reach to heights of 20,500 feet. The Eastern highlands are separated by a great valley into the northern Guiana highlands and the southern extensive tableland of Brazil. The Brazil highland is highest near the coast, and that part of it which is over 5000 feet high runs from south-west to north-east, and is equally distributed about the Tropic of Capricorn.

Aconcagua in the Andes

The plains of South America are widest in equatorial latitudes. The northern lowland is generally known as the *llanos.*   The wide, central lowland is densely forested, as its name *selvas* implies.   The southern lowlands are the only extensive lowlands outside the Tropics, and are known as the *pampas.*

Divides and Rivers.

The Andes form the great divide between the Pacific and Atlantic systems of rivers.   From them, many relatively small rivers drain to the Pacific.   The long and voluminous rivers flowing eastward to the Atlantic leave the plateaux, by gaps cut into the eastern rim. The Cauca-Magdalena, of Colombia, runs parallel to the Cordilleras for a great part of its course.

The chief Andean tributaries of the Amazon are the Marañon and Ucayali, each of which runs for some distance through the high plateau, forming a series of cataracts in its passage through the eastern rim.   The two rivers, joining at Nauta, are there at an altitude of less than 400 ft. above the sea.   The united stream, known as the Amazon, is navigable for 1,800 miles to the sea.   From the north come great rivers draining the slopes of the Colombian Andes and Guiana highlands. The chief of these rivers is the Negro.   From the south-west and south rivers drain into the Amazon from the Bolivian Andes and the Brazil highlands.   Of these rivers the chief are the Madeira and Tocantins.

It is possible to pass from the Amazon valley to the Orinoco valley over a saddle, the lowest point of which is not 600 feet high.   The upper Orinoco, which rises in the Guiana highlands, follows the western and northern edges of these highlands in a semi-circular course.   It ends its course in a large delta.   North of the Orinoco plains there runs a spur of the Andes, and from this and the main Andean chain there come many large rivers to the Orinoco.   This river is navigable for 1,000 miles.

The Paraguay-Parana has a low divide, separating it from the Amazon.   From this divide, the Paraguay runs southward to the larger Parana, which drains the western slopes of the Brazil highlands. The joint river, from Corrientes southward, is known as the Parana. East of the Parana, the Uruguay drains the south-west part of the Brazil highlands, and its estuary, the River Plate, receives the waters of the Parana near parallel 34° S. The Parana is navigable for 250 miles upstream from Corrientes ; the Paraguay almost to its source ; and the Uruguay to the Salto Cascades, $31\frac{1}{2}$° S.

Coast.

The north coast of South America is deeply indented by the Gulf of Venezuela. Bordered to the east by a series of islands, the chief of which is Trinidad (North America), the coast becomes sandy especially near the delta of the Orinoco. To the mouth of the Amazon, the coast is still a sandy plain, continuing so to Cape San Roque. Southward to the Tropic, the rocky coast is broken by several harbours, the chief of which is the Bay of Rio de Janeiro. South of the Tropic to the mouth of the Plate estuary, the coast is fringed by a series of lagoons, the largest of which empties to the sea at parallel 32° S. Several bays lie south of the Plate, and in the far south, the island of Tierra del Fuego is separated from the mainland by Magellan Strait. East of the mouth of this strait lie the much-indented Falkland Islands, the many harbours of which are used by British whalers. Magellan Strait leads westward to the fiord coast of southern Chile, where there is beautiful scenery. North of Chiloe Island, the coast is rocky and almost unbroken. Its few harbours are open to the north. The Gulf of Guayaquil, nearly 200 miles south of the Equator, is the only large gulf on the Pacific coast.

Climate.

(a) Air-temperatures.

The greater part of South America lies within that belt of the Earth's surface in which every place receives the Sun's vertical rays at noon for two days each year. The equatorial lands receive the greatest heat from the Sun at the end of June and December, while in March and September, they receive as much heat as we do in our summer. Thus their air-temperatures are never low. Northward, the summer season occurs from May to August, and southward, around the Tropic of Capricorn, December and January are the hottest months. South of the Tropic, the sun's heating power diminishes at all seasons in a southerly direction, and with it the average air-temperatures also become lower. The high altitudes attained by the Cordilleras and the highlands give to parts of the western republics, to the Guianas, and to Brazil low air-temperatures. Thus, Quito, 9,000 ft. above sea-level, has a mean annual air-temperature of 55½° F. ; Para, receiving similar heat from the Sun, but at sea-level, has a mean annual temperature of 80° F.

(b) Rainfall.

At all seasons the air over the Amazon basin is rising into regions of lower temperature. This movement causes the air to be cooled and saturated with water vapour. Consequently large amounts of rain fall in the Amazon basin. Southward the rainfall gradually becomes less. Patagonia, swept by land breezes, receives little rain. The mighty Andes play an important part in the distribution of the rainfall. The inflowing winds are forced up the steep Andean slopes, and are so saturated with water vapour, because of the cooling brought about, that they shed all their water on the eastern slopes of the ranges. Little chance is there for the leeward slopes to receive rain from the high-level winds, which pass over the Cordilleras. Where these winds sink down, they become warmer and unsaturated. The low-level winds which sweep the Pacific coasts in January are generally warming on their northward journey and shed little or no rain.

In July America south of the Equator and east of

the Andes receives little rain except near the coasts. The south-west Pacific slopes of the Andes receive cooling west winds, from which by the influence of the Andes rain falls in large amounts. This region has therefore a climate like that of the Mediterranean. North of parallel 30° S. and south of the Equator, the Pacific coastal plains and slopes receive practically no rain. North of the Gulf of Guayaquil the rainfall increases. The Orinoco basin and the eastern parts of the Guianas have their chief rainy season at this time of the year.

It will be noticed that the Pacific coasts from Guayaquil southward to parallel 30° S. are practically rainless. The intermontane plateaux of the Andes are also regions of low rainfall from this gulf southwards ; and the low rainfall belt widens southward, ending in the Atlantic coast between parallels 40° S. and 50° S.

Plants and Animals.

In the extreme south, which is well watered, there are forests of beech and pine. East of the Andes, the decreasing rainfall and increasing air-temperatures cause a dwarfing of these trees, until the land becomes a steppe west of the River Plate. Trees of an evergreen type grow in the river valleys. Further north, near the Tropic, the eastern well-watered coastal lands are covered with dense forests, producing rosewood, dye-woods, and Araucarian pine. Westward the lower rainfall produces park lands, or savanas, which lead to a more wooded region—the Matto Grosso, or great woods.

In the Amazon basin the heavy rainfall along with the great heat produces one of the densest wooded regions in the world. Trees grow rapidly and their lower parts are covered by dense undergrowth, making exploration in these districts laborious and very slow. These *selvas* cover an enormous area—nearly as large as Europe ; and from them rubber, ornamental and dye woods, palms and bamboos are obtained. The selvas

reach far up the eastern slopes of the Andes ; and in
Ecuador and Peru the cinchona tree (from whose bark
quinine is obtained) grows wild.

North and west of the main stream of the Orinoco,
there is another region of savanas. The great *llanos*,
as these parts are called, are grass regions with scattered
clumps of trees.

On the west coast, the southern part of South America
is well watered (especially in winter) and is wooded.
North of about parallel 30° S., vegetation is practically
non-existent, except in the higher parts of the Andes.
On the Peruvian coast, south of the Gulf of Guayaquil,
the rivers supply water from the high Andes to the dry
plains ; and vegetation of a tropical type clothes the
river banks. North of Guayaquil, there is a thick
growth of tropical vegetation.

The savanas are the natural haunts of the larger
wild animals, some of which are vegetable feeders while
others are carnivorous. The puma (mountain lion) and
jaguar represent the 'big cats.' The tapir of the
tropical forests and the great ant-eater are other
interesting mammals. The representatives of the 'Old
World' camel in this country are the llama, alpaca, and
vicuna. The condor, boa-constrictor, turtle and alligator
are also noteworthy.

Agriculture and Pasture.

The lands available for agriculture are not extensive,
when compared with the vast size of the continent.
The thick growth of trees in the selvas prevents any
agricultural operations. The eastern parts of the savanas
and steppes are the lands most suitable for agriculture.
Their western parts are pastoral lands. The cooler
parts of the continent, south of the Tropic, are in their
coastal portions producers of maize. The lower Parana
valley and the land lying west of the Plate estuary are
wheat producing. Chile, from latitude 30° S. to its fiord
coast, has similar crops, and its clear summer skies and
winter rains allow Mediterranean type of fruits to be

cultivated. The warmer, coastal lands of the tropical belt produce coffee, sugar, tobacco, and cotton. In the north-west, from the coasts of Ecuador to Venezuela, cacao, coffee, cotton, and tobacco are cultivated. On the plateaux of Colombia, Ecuador, Peru, and Bolivia, wheat and barley are grown for local consumption.

The chief pastoral districts are the Orinoco and Paraguay-Parana basins. The eastern parts of Argentine and the west of Uruguay are great cattle-rearing districts, and the drier, western parts of Argentine are being used as feeding grounds for sheep. Llamas and alpacas are bred for their wool in the higher parts of Peru.

Minerals.

The Andes, throughout their entire length, have valuable outcrops of mineral veins. *Gold* is worked in Colombia and Ecuador, and *silver* and *tin* in Bolivia. Brazil has *coal*-fields in its southern states, and *gold*, and *diamonds* in the state of Minas Geraes. The Guiana highlands are rich in gold. The Atacama desert of north Chile yields large quantities of sodium nitrate (Chile saltpetre).

Colombia.

Position and Surface.

The north-western portion of this country is separated from Central America by a short land boundary, and it is washed by the Atlantic and Pacific Oceans. Its southern border is, roughly, the Equator, and its area is about 3½ times that of the British Isles. From the coasts there is a steep rise up to the western range of the Cordilleras. The Magdalena-Cauca runs parallel to the 'grain' of the country, northward between three of the ranges; and the eastern range has steep slopes leading down to the Orinoco-Negro basins. The Cordillera between the Cauca-Magdalena valleys has several snow-clad volcanic cones ; and this range is prolonged, north of the Magdalena gap, to a snowy coast range between the Magdalena and the Gulf of Venezuela.

Climate and Productions.

The whole country comes under the influence of the Sun's vertical rays, but the high altitudes of the Cordilleras and of their valleys create much lower air-temperatures. Rain falls west of the Cordilleras in two rainy seasons ; and in the low, eastern parts the chief rains fall in the first half of the year. The lower parts of the Cordilleran slopes produce sugar, cacao, and other tropical products ; the intermediate zone produces coffee and maize ; and in the higher parts, wheat grows. In the east the plains are separable into a northern savana part (used for grazing cattle), and a southern part occupied by selvas (which yield rubber and dye-woods). *Gold, emeralds,* and *silver* are worked in the mountains ; and there are valuable pearl fisheries in the Caribbean Sea.

Communications and Towns.

The Magdalena, navigable for 500 miles, forms the chief means of communication. *Puerto Colombia* lies at the mouth of the Magdalena ; *Bogota* (8,000 ft.) is the capital. There are over 5 million people in the Republic. Their chief exports are coffee, skins, bananas, and rubber. The chief imports are flour, lard, petroleum, and cotton goods.

Venezuela.

Position and Surface.

East of the main Andes, and south of the Caribbean Sea, lies the republic of Venezuela, which is three times as large as our islands. A great part of this country lies in the Orinoco basin. On the north, between the Orinoco llanos and the sea, there runs a large range of mountains, continuous in the west with the Andes. The western part of the Guiana highlands is included in

The Falls on the Orinoco near Canasto, Venezuela

Venezuela and is drained by the Orinoco. The lowlands north of this river are savanas, supporting 2 million oxen and half as many pigs. Goats are reared on the hill-slopes, the seaward slopes of which are covered with coffee plantations; and near the coastal lowlands cacao and sugar are grown. Famous *gold* mines occur in the Guiana highlands, and there are also productive *copper* mines.

Industries and Towns.

Of the population, which does not number 3 millions, one-fifth is engaged in agriculture. Pastoral industries are the more important, cattle and hides being exported. A railway from the port of *La Guaira* climbs the coastal mountains to *Caracas*, the capital. From Caracas, which lies in a cacao-producing district, the line continues westward to *Valencia*, the centre of a coffee-growing district. The chief imports of this Republic are manufactured articles, and the exports coffee, cacao, sugar, rubber, hides, cattle, and gold.

Ecuador.

General Features and Productions.

From the Pacific slopes Ecuador narrows inland, and has a width from west to east of 15°. The country is slightly less in size than the British Isles, and has a population of 2 million people. Three well-marked districts make up the surface of the country. The Pacific coastal district is hot, wet, and unhealthy. Around the Gulf of Guayaquil, large amounts of cacao are grown; and coffee-plantations are important at higher altitudes. The Andes, narrow, high, and steep-sided on the west and on the east, form the second district, which has low air-temperatures and moderate rainfall. The high plateaux between the western and eastern ranges support only a scanty vegetation, wheat and barley being grown for local consumption. The third and largest district occupies the eastern slopes of the Andes, which drain to the Amazon. These slopes are covered by selvas producing valuable woods, rubber, and cinchona bark.

The Andes, which are crowned by some of the highest snow-clad volcanic cones in the world (Chimborazo and Cotopaxi being 20,500 feet above sea-level), are rich in precious metals.

People, Communications, and Towns.

The majority of the people of Ecuador are pure Indians. Europeans of pure blood are few. The making of Panama hats is the chief industry other than agriculture. There are also some flour-mills, sugar works, and chocolate factories. *Quito*, the capital, is connected with the larger town of *Guayaquil*, its seaport, by a short railway line. In the high passes of the plateaux, the llama is used as a beast of burden. Cacao is the main export, and textiles and food-stuffs are the chief imports.

Peru.

General Features.

The Republic of Peru controls a long coast-line, from Guayaquil to the point where the coast runs in a north-south direction. The country has physical features similar to those of Ecuador, but its intermontane plateaux are wider. From these many rivers cut through the western Cordillera to the Pacific ; and the mighty head streams of the Amazon drain through the eastern rim on their long journey to the Atlantic. Peru claims the valleys of these rivers, as well as part of the Amazon proper. In the south, the Republic includes the north-western part of L. Titicaca. The area of Peru is 6 times that of the British Isles.

Climate and Productions.

The hot season of Peru is the beginning and end of the solar year. During the hot season the Amazon slopes of this country receive heavy rain, while the Pacific slopes are swept by cold and dry south winds. In winter the Pacific slopes are bathed in mists, from which drizzling rains fall.

The coast region is practically desert, except along the rivers. Irrigation works are in operation, making it possible to cultivate cotton, cacao, and sugar in this district. In the Andes and in the plateaux, there are many fertile valleys; it is in this belt that the llama, alpaca, and vicuna are reared for their wool. The Amazon slopes present a striking contrast to these other regions. In their lowest parts selvas clothe the hillsides, leading upward as the air-temperatures decrease to cooler types of trees and finally to treeless regions. The selvas are rich in rubber. Mining operations are being carried on in the high plateaux, *gold, silver,* and *copper* being obtained. *Guano* is dug in the coastal regions.

People and Towns.

Two-thirds of the four million people of Peru are Indians. From the ports of *Callao* and *Mollendo* railway lines run to the plateaux. The line from *Mollendo,* through *Arequipa* to L. Titicaca, runs north-west to *Cuzco,* and along the south-east shores of L. Titicaca to Bolivian territory. *Callao,* the chief port, is connected with *Lima,* the capital, by electric railway ; and from the capital, a line runs to the mining town of *Pasco.* Metals and minerals, sugar, raw cotton, guano, and wool form the chief exports. The imports are chiefly manufactured goods and coal.

Bolivia.

Surface and Productions.

Bolivia, 4 times as large as the British Isles, is the most isolated republic of South America. It has no coast line, and its nearest ports lie on the Peruvian and Chilian coasts. Part of the country is a high plateau, containing half of L. Titicaca and also L. Aullagas into which Titicaca drains. The plains east

Lima

of this lake bear crops of potatoes and barley, and are pasture lands for cattle, llamas and sheep. Eastward the plains lead up to high Cordilleras, in which there are valuable mineral veins producing one-quarter of the world's output of *tin*, as well as *silver, copper*, and other valuable minerals. The eastern slopes of this mountain range are drained by the Mamore which is known in Brazil as the Madeira, and by the Pilcomayo which runs to the Paraguay. These rich valleys yield cinchona and coffee; and their lower parts, in the selvas region, are rich in rubber. Cacao and coffee are grown near La Paz, south-east of L. Titicaca.

People, Communications, and Towns.

The population numbers nearly 3 millions, of whom half are Indians. Half the working population is agricultural. To counteract its natural isolation, Bolivia's republican government has constructed several hundred miles of railway, the chief line of which runs from Antofagasta on the Chile coast, north-east to the eastern shores of L. Aullagas, and through *Oruro* to *La Paz*, the capital. A shorter line runs from Arica (Chile) north-east to La Paz. Lines also run to the Argentine Republic. The chief exports of Bolivia are tin and rubber; and the chief imports are provisions, hardware, and manufactured goods.

Chile.

Surface, Climate, and Productions.

The Pacific coastal plains and slopes of the Andes, from parallel 18° S. to their termination in the island of Tierra del Fuego, are under the control of the republic of Chile. This long country has an average width, from west to east, of 100 miles, and an area more than twice that of the British Isles. The coast is regular from the Peruvian border as far as parallel 41° S., and afterwards it becomes a fiord coast, fringed by islands. A submerged saddle, Magellan Strait, separates the mainland from Tierra del Fuego.

For about 6° on either side of the Tropic of Capricorn, Chile is a hot land with no rainfall ; and so this hot region is a great desert—the Atacama desert. The whole region is rich in nitrates, especially in sodium nitrate (Chile saltpetre). *Iquique* is the chief port for trade in nitrates. South of parallel 30° S., and north of the fiord coast, the less heated land is relatively dry in summer but it receives heavy winter rains. Mediterranean types of fruits, and wheat, are cultivated among the clearings of the evergreen trees. The grass regions of this zone support over 4 million sheep, and half as many cattle. Dairy-farming is increasing in importance. Southward, in the fiord district, rain falls at all seasons, and deciduous and coniferous forests continue as far as the terminal island. South of parallel 37° S. there is an area one-tenth the size of the British Isles, in which lumbering and the manufacture of wood-pulp are becoming very important industries. Sheep-farming is the chief occupation in the clearings of this wooded zone. In the Cordilleras there are veins of *copper, gold* and *silver* ores. *Coal* outcrops south-east of Concepcion.

People and Towns.

Four million people are ruled by the republican government. Of these, about 3 °/₀ are Indians.

Railways run from the ports of *Arica* and *Antofagasta* to Bolivia; and from the latter town a railway runs south through *Valparaiso*, the port of *Santiago*, the capital, to *Concepcion, Valdivia*, and the head of the fiord coast. Valparaiso is connected eastward with the Trans-Andine line which runs *via* the Uspallata pass and tunnel, south of Aconcagua, to the Argentine. The chief trade of Chile is with the United States of America. Nitrates and copper are sent to our islands, and cotton and woollen goods are received in return.

Argentine.

Surface, Climate, and Productions.

Argentine is over nine times as large as the United Kingdom. The Andes on the west, the Atlantic Ocean and the river Uruguay on the east, and the Parana, Paraguay and Pilcomayo on the north are its boundaries. The northern and hottest part of the country is occupied by the Paraguay-Parana basin, and is a well wooded region. Southwards, 'scrub' vegetation leads to grassy plains, or *pampas*, the equivalent of the European steppes. Their eastern, better-watered parts are great maize- and wheat-growing lands, especially in the state of Buenos Aires; and their drier, western and southern parts are the pasture ground of sheep. Cattle graze in millions in the richer grass lands between the rivers. The upland state of Mendoza is a vine-growing district; and the slopes of the Andes, as far as Tierra del Fuego, are forest-clad. Precious metals outcrop in various parts of the Argentine.

People and Towns.

Eight million people are all this vast country supports. Pastoral and agricultural industries are the chief means of livelihood; and industries depending on these are increasing in importance. In addition to the navigable waterways, there are over 25,000 miles of railway. The lines spread out like a fan from Buenos Aires; and the chief line passes westward through Mendoza to the Trans-Andine line, leading to Valparaiso, the port of Chile. *Buenos Aires*, with 1½ million inhabitants, is the largest town in South America. It has a good artificial harbour; and it is the centre of the industrial and political life of the republic. Animals and agricultural products form the chief exports, and manufactured goods the chief imports. Nearly half Argentine's total trade is done with the United Kingdom. We receive about a sixth of our wheat supply from this country, and two-fifths of our beef and mutton supply.

Paraguay and Uruguay.

Paraguay is nearly as large as the British Isles, and has a population of a million people. It is an inland republic, bounded on the west by the Pilcomayo-Paraguay, and on the south-east by the upper Parana. It is a low-lying country, wooded in the west and swampy in the south. Paraguay has excellent grazing land, which supports large numbers of cattle. Paraguay tea, or *maté*, is extensively grown and is used throughout the continent. The woods of the Gran Chaco yield valuable timber, and orange groves are important. Meat, timber, and maté form the chief exports; and textiles the chief imports. *Asuncion* is the capital and river port to which come vessels from the Plate estuary.

Uruguay is a much smaller country, lying east of the river Uruguay and stretching to the Atlantic Ocean on the south and east. In an area, about half that of the British Isles, there are 1½ million people, who are chiefly engaged in rearing sheep, cattle and horses in the extensive grass regions of the country.

The cultivation of wheat and maize is increasing. *Monte Video*, the capital of the republic, *Fray Bentos*, and *Paysandu* have large meat-packing yards, from which beef, ox-tongues, and meat extracts are exported.

Brazil.

Surface and Productions.

The United States of Brazil have a total area a little less than that of the United States of America. Bounded by a coast-line of 4,000 miles on the east, Brazil has a land boundary which touches ten other countries. Its greatest width is along parallel 7° S., in the Amazon basin. Its south-east part is mountainous, especially near that part of the coast which is cut by the Tropic of Capricorn. Excepting its three southern states, Brazil lies within the Tropics ; but its eastern highlands give to the states of Pernambuco, Goyaz, Minas Geraes and Sao Paulo almost temperate conditions. The Amazon lowland is very hot and receives heavy summer rains. Selvas, with impenetrable undergrowths of climbing plants, cover thousands of square miles of the interior, and yield rubber, ornamental- and dye-woods, cacao and vanilla. In the eastern coastal states near the Tropic, four-fifths of the world's output of coffee is grown. The states north of the R. Sao Francisco produce cotton and sugar, and south of that river tobacco is grown.

The chief mineral district is the upper Sao Francisco valley, in the state of Minas Geraes. *Diamonds, gold, coal,* and *iron* are the chief minerals.

People, Trade, and Towns.

It is estimated that 30 million people inhabit the republic of Brazil. Portuguese form the chief European element ; but in the south there is a colony of Germans. The Amazon is the chief waterway, but the selvas prevent much immigration to its basin. Railways are being constructed in all parts of the Brazil highlands, chiefly from the ports to the productive hinterlands.

The chief exports of Brazil are coffee, sugar and rubber. The United States of America receive most of Brazil's exports. The United Kingdom sends manufactures and coal to Brazil, receiving rubber, raw cotton and coffee from this republic. *Rio de Janeiro* (population 1 million) is the capital and chief port. *Santos, Bahia, Pernambuco,* and *Para* are other great ports.

The Guianas.

North of Brazil, and east of Venezuela, lie three colonies which stretch southward from low swampy plains, washed by the Atlantic Ocean, to the Guiana highlands. Sugar, cacao, rice, maize, and bananas are cultivated. *Gold* mining is an important industry in the highlands. As the lowlands are hot and very damp in summer, the sugar plantations are worked by East Indians, over 100,000 of whom have been hired as labourers on the plantations of British Guiana. French Guiana is over one-fourth, Dutch Guiana one-third, and British Guiana three-fourths the size of the British Isles. The French colony has less than 50,000 inhabitants, of whom 10 $^{\circ}/_{\circ}$ are convicts; and Dutch Guiana has 100,000 inhabitants. There are nearly 300,000 inhabitants in the largest and best developed colony, British Guiana, the capital of which is *Georgetown*. British Guiana exports 100,000 tons of cane-sugar annually. The Falkland Is. (lat. 52° S., long. 60° W.) and British Guiana are the only parts of South America which belong to the British Empire.

QUESTIONS AND EXERCISES

Chapter I. The Shape and Size of the Earth

1. What common object has a shape like that of the Earth? Using such an object, illustrate the movements of the Earth.

2. By what means do we fix the position of a place on the globe? Distinguish between the two kinds of lines used for this purpose.

3. The longitude of Cambridge is 0° 7′ E. ; its latitude is 52° 12′ N. Explain these statements.

4. What is Standard Time? At what rate does the time vary from place to place? Standing at the globe, look over the brass meridian and slowly rotate the globe. Name the time at each of the meridians marked on the globe, supposing it is 9 a.m. Wednesday on the Greenwich meridian.

5. How are the position and relief of a place shown on a map?

6. In your own words describe the method by which to survey a country.

Chapter II. The Atmosphere

1. How does the air get its heat, and how is the temperature of the air measured?

2. Explain fully why the Sun has greater heating power in the northern hemisphere during July than during December.

3. Put a small stone and an equal weight of water (contained in a test-tube) into boiling water. Withdraw these after a short time, and allow them to cool in the air. Which cools the more quickly? What lesson may be learned from this?

4. Why are high mountains snow-clad, even within the Tropics? Name some of these snow-clad peaks.

5. Boil some water in a kettle. Sketch what you see coming out of the spout. Put your finger in the grey cloud; and in the space between the cloud and the spout. Is the cloud made of liquid or gas?

6. What is wind? How are winds named? Explain why a north wind is cold and why a south wind is warm in England.

7. From what quarter do the rain-shedding winds of the British Isles come? Why do they shed their rain?

8. Name, and describe the position of, an island in the trade wind belt. Describe the chief features of the weather experienced in it. Compare them with those of the weather in an island in the west wind belt (e.g. Ireland).

CHAPTER III. LIFE ON THE EARTH'S SURFACE

1. Account for the desert condition of so large a part of Africa.

2. What kinds of trees would you expect to find in Canada, South France, Ceylon, Sweden, Central Africa, Japan?

3. Give two examples of important cultivated plants which are grown only in the Tropics; describe the kind of climate which favours each, and name a region in which each is produced.

4. In what vegetation regions would you find the following:—zebra, penguin, a fur-bearing animal, ape, boa-constrictor, kangaroo?

5. Copy from Whitaker's Almanac a list of the large towns of the British Isles. Find how many of these lie on or near coalfields.

CHAPTER IV. EUROPE

1. Compare the advantages and disadvantages which the Mediterranean and Baltic seas present to the navigator.

2. On an outline map of Europe, insert and name the seven large mountain ranges of Europe. Name also the Plain of Lombardy and the Plain of Hungary.

3. Name in order the countries which touch the Baltic Sea; and give the names and positions of two gulfs and two islands in that sea.

4. Compare the Rhine with the Rhone. Illustrate your answer by a sketch map of each river.

5. Cork, London, Dresden, and Kief are nearly in the same latitude. What are the differences of climate between these places, and how do you account for these differences?

6. Compare the summer and winter rainfall of north Europe with that of south Europe.

7. On a political map of Europe mark the limits of the coniferous, deciduous, and evergreen tree zones. What vegetation is there in eastern Russia?

8. In what parts of Europe are the following minerals raised: lead, petroleum, gold, graphite, sulphur?

The British Isles

1. Explain the terms, British Isles, United Kingdom, Great Britain.

2. Make a list of the rivers which flow through gaps (*a*) in the Limestone hills, (*b*) in the Chiltern hills, (*c*) in the hills which separate Strathmore and its continuation from the central lowlands of Scotland.

3. On an outline map of Ireland shade the highlands, naming each. Locate the most important gaps, with the rivers running through each.

4. Find the average range of temperature from July to January in (*a*) south-west Ireland, (*b*) eastern Ireland, (*c*) north Wales, (*d*) East Anglia, (*e*) north Scotland.

5. Construct a diagrammatic section across the Pennine chain from west to east. Suppose that a west wind is blowing over this section. Where will the air be saturated? What will result from this saturation?

6. In what parts of the British Isles would you expect to find (a) agricultural, (b) pastoral, industries as the mainstay of the people?

7. State and explain the reasons why the eastern counties of England are specially adapted for the cultivation of wheat.

8. Arrange the four countries of the British Islands in order of importance as regards mineral wealth. How has the presence or absence of coal affected each country?

9. Give the position and extent of two of the most important English coalfields; name two towns situated in each of these districts, and mention their special industries.

10. Where are the chief iron mines in the British Isles? From what countries is iron now imported (either as ore or pig) to our furnaces?

11. Draw a map of the West Riding of Yorkshire. Name the large towns in this district, and in each valley the chief industry. What has helped in the building up of these industries?

12. 'Nearly 90% of the world's clothing is made of cotton goods.' How does this affect the British Isles?

13. Name towns in which the following are the chief industries: silk, pottery, linen, 'straw' hats, chemicals.

14. On an outline map of the British Isles mark the position of, and name, the chief ports. From each port draw in ink an arrow, and at the point of this arrow write the name of the chief export. Draw another arrow in pencil, pointing to each port. At the tail of this, write the name of the chief import.

15. What advantages do London, Glasgow, and Cardiff gain from their situation? Choose any three of the Universities in the United Kingdom (other than London and Glasgow); give the position of each, and state the chief industrial occupation of the district surrounding each.

16.   Make a large plan (*vide* a railway guide) of the chief docks of the Port of London Authority.

France

1.   On a contour map of France, name the Languedoc saddle, Doubs-Rhône saddle, Moselle gap, and also the chief highlands and valleys.   How does each of the three first mentioned features affect French commerce and politics ?

2.   Draw an outline of the coasts of the English Channel. Locate and name the chief packet and naval stations on each side of the channel.

3.   How does the rainfall of France vary (*a*) seasonally, (*b*) regionally ?

4.   Enumerate the chief industries of the French people. Which of these are dependent for the greater amount of their raw material on foreign countries ?

5.   Describe the position, relief, and natural resources of Alsace-Lorraine.

6.   Describe the geographical conditions which have led to the growth or decay of: Paris, Rouen, Havre, Roubaix, Lyons, Nice, Metz.

Belgium

1.   Measure the length of the coast-line of Belgium. What river's mouth is more important to this country than the coast ?

2.   Of the rivers Scheldt and Meuse, which would be easier to navigate upstream ?   In what way have the Belgians improved their inland navigation ?

3.   Compare the crops of Belgium with those of England in the same latitudes.

4.   In what part of Belgium is the population most densely gathered ?   Explain the geographical conditions which are the causes of this.

5.   By what routes is it possible to travel from London to Liège ?

6.   Name five large Belgian towns ; describe the position of each and the industries of the inhabitants of each town.

Holland

1. What is a delta? Explain the terms dyke and polder.

2. Name the characteristic agricultural and pastoral products of this country.

3. From what parts of the world do the Dutch get coffee and diamonds?

4. Why is Amsterdam so large a city? What is its rival? Name their packet stations.

Germany

1. What countries surround Germany? In each case, state whether the boundary runs along low or high land. What changes have occurred since the signing of the Treaty of Versailles?

2. To what point is the Rhine navigable, (*a*) for ocean steamers, (*b*) for river steamers? Is the Elbe equally navigable?

3. Compare the two portions of the German coast-line. Which is the more valuable? Describe two routes along which to navigate a large vessel from one coast to the other.

4. Compare the air-temperatures and rainfall of (i) west and east Germany, (ii) north and south Germany.

5. What are the chief crops, other than cereals, grown in Germany? To what uses are these put?

6. Is more or less coal produced from the German coalfields than from the British coalfields? Name one German coalfield, and two towns on it.

7. Where would you go in order to study the conditions of life of German factory 'hands' engaged in (*a*) silk, (*b*) wool, (*c*) steel, and (*d*) clothing, trades?

8. To what causes do you attribute the growth of Hamburg, Berlin, Cologne, Elberfeld, Munich?

Denmark

1. Describe two interesting natural phenomena which may be studied in the Danish Empire.

2. Has Denmark more or less rainfall than European countries in the same latitudes? How does the Baltic Sea affect Denmark's climate (*a*) in summer, (*b*) in winter?

3. What Danish products are sold daily in English markets? What is the chief port from which they come?

Scandinavia

1. Draw a large map of Sweden south of parallel 60° N. Name the three great lakes and show which way their waters drain to the sea. What uses have been made of these lakes?

2. Contrast the west and east coasts of Scandinavia. In what way do the shapes of each, and the salinity of the surrounding seas, affect navigation?

3. To what town, and in what country, would you go to observe the 'midnight sun'?

4. What is 'deal'? From which part of this peninsula do we get the greater part of our supply of deal?

5. 'Pig iron' is imported at Hull, and floated up the Don. From what district do the ore and 'pig' come? To what place do they go?

Russia

1. Describe the relief of Russia. What influence has it on the utility of the rivers?

2. Distinguish between (*a*) tundra, (*b*) the 'black earth' region, (*c*) steppes.

3. Examine the daily newspaper reports of the London Markets; and compare the prices of Russian wheat and barley with those from other sources.

4. Name the chief towns where the following are the industries : (*a*) coal-mining, (*b*) cotton-spinning, (*c*) commerce, (*d*) exportation of timber, (*e*) exportation of wheat.

Poland

1. Describe the position and relief of Poland by drawing a sketch map. Mark the position of the coalfield, and of Warsaw and Lodz.

2. Write a short history of Poland, from the 14th century onward.

3. What are the chief industries of Poland? By what routes does Poland carry on its external trade?

The Central Republics

1. Make a list of the countries which adjoin Czecho-Slovakia, Austria and Hungary. Which is the most powerful of these?

2. Examine a large contour map of the provinces of Upper and Lower Austria ; and describe and account for the position of the chief towns in these provinces.

3. Compare the industries of Czecho-Slovakia with those of Hungary. How far is the climate of each country responsible for these industries?

4. Trace the courses of the chief railway lines which run from Vienna to (a) Italy, (b) Constantinople, (c) Bukarest. Notice the relief of the country through which each railway passes.

5. Name the industries of Vienna, Budapest, Graz, Brno, and Prague.

The Balkan Peninsula

1. Along what valleys do the chief railways of the Balkan Peninsula run?

2. Name the natural products of this region, and the industries supported by these.

3. Rumania is sometimes mentioned in the commercial news of the daily newspaper. In what connection?

4. Make a list of the chief ports of the Balkan Peninsula, and the countries controlling each port?

5. What changes have taken place recently as a result of the War of 1914–18?

Switzerland

1. Describe the relief of Switzerland. In which part are there most towns? In what way do the other relief zones affect these towns?

2. Account for the great proportion of waste land in Switzerland. What are alps? How much of the country is forested?

3. How do the Swiss get power for their factories? Name some of the products of these factories.

Italy

1. Trace a map of Italy, and mark on it (i) the new boundaries, (ii) the old boundaries, (iii) the 600 ft. contour line, (iv) the chief railway routes.

2. Compare and contrast the natural vegetation of Italy with that of the British Isles. Why is there this difference between the vegetation of these kingdoms?

3. Describe (i) a volcanic cone, (ii) a glacier, (iii) the effect of an earthquake. What effect has each of these on the occupations of the Italians?

4. Draw sketch maps showing the positions of Rome, Milan, Trieste.

The Iberian Peninsula

1. In what time zone do Portugal and Spain lie? What time is it at Constantinople when the Madrid clocks indicate 3 p.m. ?

2. On as large a scale as possible, draw a map of the Iberian Peninsula. Name capes Finisterre, Roca, Tarifa; Trafalgar Bay. Mark and name the Castilian Mts., and the Sierra Morena; the rivers Douro, Ebro, and Tagus; Barcelona, Bilbao, Corunna, Granada, Lisbon, Oporto, Seville.

3. Account for the small rainfall of the Spanish plateau.

4. In what parts of the Iberian peninsula would you expect to find the following industries practised : pastoral, iron-ore mining, wine-making, orange growing?

5. Compare Lisbon with Madrid as regards (a) position, (b) range of air-temperatures, (c) industries.

CHAPTER V. ASIA

1. Name the chief peninsulas and island groups of Asia.

2. Describe the easiest routes across the Asiatic continent. What effects have the rims of the plateaux on trade routes?

3. Name the four great Asiatic rivers indicated as follows :

(i) The western river of the Siberian plain.

(ii) The great highway of Central China.

(iii) The twin rivers of Mesopotamia.

Describe the nature of the country traversed by each—as mountain or plain, forest, grass region, or desert.

4. Using the maps showing the January and July rainfall of Asia, write a short description of the amount and seasonal distribution of the rainfall in that part of Asia which lies south of parallel 40° N.

5. What parts of Asia produce large crops of summer wheat, winter wheat, teak, tea, sugar, figs, cotton?

6. State (i) why Bombay derived greater advantage than Calcutta from the making of the Suez Canal, (ii) from what ports of Asia large supplies of cotton, silk, rice, tobacco and tea are exported to Great Britain and other European countries.

Siberia, Caucasia, and Turkestan

1. What do you know of the range in air-temperatures, and the seasonal distribution of the rainfall, in western Siberia and Trans-Caucasia?

2. Name the pastoral and agricultural products of Siberia which are imported into the British Isles.

3. Make a list of the Asiatic oil-shares mentioned in the commercial section of the daily newspaper. At what ports is the oil taken on board?

4. Draw a map showing the chief railways in this region. Mark the positions of the important towns on those lines.

Japan

1. Compare the depth of the sea-floor to the east and to the west of Honshiu.

2. Describe the position, relief, and climate of Japan, accounting as fully as you can for its climate. Compare the British Isles with Japan in these respects.

3. What are the advantages and disadvantages of Japanese rivers? Compare the directions of the rivers with the chief railway routes.

4. Name the modern industries which the Japanese have learned from west Europe ; and state where these industries are carried on.

5. What British industries and towns are likely to be affected by the imports and exports of Japan ?

China

1. ' The Chinese Empire lies in latitudes similar to those of the Mediterranean Sea and North Africa.' What differences exist between the climates of these districts, and why are there these differences?

2. Draw a large map of the Yang-tse-kiang basin. Name each important tributary. What do you learn from this map concerning the influence of geographical conditions on the position of a town?

3. What is the chief occupation of the Chinese? By what means do they cultivate rice and tea?

4. Why should China become in the future one of the greatest manufacturing countries in the world?

5. Name the chief European territories and ports along the Chinese coast. What influences are these districts likely to have on Chinese trade?

South-east Asia

1. What is the name for the submerged land connecting Sumatra and Borneo with the neighbouring continent? Write down the greatest depths recorded in the seas to the south of Sumatra and Java. Where is Krakatoa, and for what is it noteworthy ?

2.   Name some of the characteristic vegetable products of this district.   What is copra, and to what use is it put in England?   Notice in the daily newspaper the references to S.E. Asia under the heading 'copra.'

3.   What is the present price of tin per ton?   How many S.E. Asiatic tin companies are mentioned in the City news to-day?

4.   Make large sketch maps showing the positions of Singapore, Manila, and Batavia.

India

1.   What time is it at Delhi when it is noon at Greenwich? How much of India comes under the influence of the vertical rays of the Sun?

2.   Compare the Ganges basin with that of the Indus. State the importance of the waters of these basins to the people.

3.   Distinguish between the Malabar and Coromandel coasts, compare the position and importance of Bombay with Madras, and illustrate your answer by a carefully drawn sketch map.

4.   In what parts of India are the following to be found : dense forests, rice-growing districts, jute-growing districts, tea plantations, rubber plantations?

5.   To what use are the following animals put in India, where are they used, and for what reasons : elephant, cattle, camel?

6.   Examine a large map of India, and note an extensive district in which there are (i) very numerous towns, (ii) very few towns.   Account for these conditions.

7.   Describe the position of Delhi, Calcutta, Bombay, Rangoon, Colombo, and Peshawar ; and state what effect the position has had on the growth of each town.

The Countries of the Western Plateaux

1. Compare the size, relief, and climate of Persia and Afghanistan.

2. Why has a considerable amount of money been expended recently on irrigation works in Mesopotamia? What crops may be cultivated in this irrigated district?

3. In what directions do the chief railways of this district run? What goods are likely to be carried by these railways?

4. Write notes on the position, commerce, etc. of Jerusalem, Mecca, Teheran, Kabul, Smyrna, Aden.

5. Give a short account of each of the following: caravan, pass, salt lake, Mediterranean type of climate, Mohammed.

CHAPTER VI.   AFRICA

1. On the map of Africa insert and name the Atlas Mts., Abyssinian highlands, Ruwenzori; mark (where necessary) and name Lake Chad, Lake Tanganyika, Cape Verde, Bulawayo, Delagoa Bay, Fez, Tripoli; trace the courses of the rivers Niger and Limpopo, naming each; and draw the boundaries of British South Africa.

2. Mark on a map of England an area equal to that of Lake Victoria. What river is fed by the water flowing from this lake, and to what use has the lake been put?

3. Examine the depths of the sea-floor around the following islands: Azores, Ascension, St Helena, Zanzibar, Socotra, Perim.   Which of these are volcanic cones? Is there any connection between their position and their origin?

4. On an outline map of Africa mark by various colours the areas over which rain falls (i) all the year round, (ii) in summer, (iii) in winter. What vegetation is supported in each of these rainfall zones?

5. What minerals have played a great part in the development of Africa? Where are the chief mining districts?

6. In the case of each of the following, the Belgian Congo, Kamerun, Senegal, Sierra Leone, Zanzibar, (i) indicate as exactly as you can its position, (ii) name the power which controls it, (iii) state the nature of the climate, (iv) state the principal export.

French Africa

1. From your atlas, trace a map of Africa and on it mark the boundaries of the French territories. Shade these in, and name each.

2. What are the important vegetable products of (i) The Barbary States, (ii) French Congo, (iii) Madagascar?

3. By what means have the French developed the Barbary States? Name the chief ports of these States.

British Africa

1. In what time zone are the capitals of (i) Province of the Cape of Good Hope, (ii) Natal, (iii) Nyasaland?

2. On an outline map of Africa on which there are marked the boundaries of the countries, mark and name the British territories. Also indicate the position and name the capitals and ports of each territory.

3. Which parts of British Africa are best suited as regards climate for British immigrants? By what means do the British keep in good health in the other territories?

4. Where are the chief pasture districts of British Africa? Name the characteristic vegetable products of each of the British territories in Africa.

5. What is banket? In what parts of Africa does banket outcrop? Name the large towns near these outcrops.

6. Describe the railway systems either of the Union of South Africa or of Uganda, Kenya Colony and Tanganyika Territory. Illustrate your answer by a sketch map.

7. From what parts of British Africa do we get mohair, coffee, ostrich feathers, cloves, ground nuts, cotton, sugar?

Egypt and the Anglo-Egyptian Sudan

1. Draw a map of the Nile basin. Mark the positions of the cataracts and of the chief barrages across the river. Also mark the courses of the railways and the positions of the chief towns.

2. How does the lower Nile get its flood water? To what uses were the flood waters put by the Egyptians, and what changes have been made by British Engineers?

3. What are the ports of the Suez Canal?

4. Say what you can of (*a*) sudd, (*b*) oasis, (*c*) bedouin, (*d*) the Pyramids.

CHAPTER ·VII.   AUSTRALIA AND NEW ZEALAND

Australia

1. On a map of Australia mark the boundaries of the six divisions, and name them. Mark and name the Great Dividing range, Flinders range, Darling range. Trace the course of and name the Swan and Murray. Mark (where necessary) and name: Gulf of St Vincent, Port Jackson, Lake Eyre, Adelaide, Ballarat, Brisbane, Fremantle, Hobart, Newcastle.

2. Describe, with a sketch map, the Murray basin. What drawbacks are there to the navigation of this river by ocean-going vessels?

3. What are coral polyps? State the conditions which are suited to the growth of reef-building corals. How does the Great Barrier Reef affect navigation?

4. Australia may be divided into four climatic belts (i) north-east, (ii) east central, (iii) south, (iv) interior. Describe each of these, and liken them to climatic zones in Europe and Africa.

5. What vegetable products of Australia are of commercial importance? Are any of the native animals of commercial importance?

6. Captain Phillip, commanding the fleet which founded the first colony in 'New South Wales' in 1788, landed at Sydney Cove 7 horses, 6 cows, 29 sheep, 12 pigs, and some poultry. Find how many of each of these there are now in Australia.

7. What minerals attracted large numbers of people to Australia, and at what date was there the great influx? Where were the minerals found, and where are they worked now?

8. Give the official titles of the large British possessions in (i) North America, (ii) South Africa, (iii) Australia. How is the King represented in these countries, and by what means are the countries governed ?

9. State (i) the chief sheep-producing district,

(ii) „   „   wine and raisin district, and

(iii) „   „   wheat district of Australia.

10. In what state are the following minerals raised : silver, tin, copper, coal ? Name the ports of each mineral district mentioned.

11. Describe the climate and natural productions of Tasmania.

12. Where are the following, and for what are they noted : Sydney, Launceston, Mildura, Boulder, Cobar, Brisbane, Adelaide, Melbourne ?

New Zealand

1. From your map determine the meridians and parallels within which New Zealand lies. Compare its position with that of the British Isles. With what European countries does New Zealand compare as regards latitude ?

2. Which of the two places, Hokitika and Christchurch, has the greater rainfall, and why is this so ? Account for the fact that the mean annual range in air-temperature of Wellington is 27° F., whereas in Vienna it is 80° F.

3. What natural phenomena may be studied in New Zealand ? To what uses, and by whom, are some of these put ?

4. Where are there extensive areas of (i) forest, (ii) sheep pastures, (iii) snow-clad mountains, in New Zealand ?

5. On an outline map of New Zealand name and mark the position of : Bay of Plenty, Cook Strait, Banks Peninsula, Stewart Island, Hauraki Gulf, Mts. Egmont and Cook ; Lakes Taupo, and Wakatipu ; the rivers Clutha and Waikato ; Auckland, Christchurch, Dunedin, and Napier.

6. What changes are made in reckoning time when going by ship (a) from New Zealand eastward across the Pacific Ocean, (b) across the Pacific Ocean westward to New Zealand ?

CHAPTER VIII. NORTH AMERICA

1. Divide North America into Time Zones. What is the value of these zones?

2. On a map of North America, insert and name the Sierra Madre, Cascade range, Appalachians. Mark (where necessary) and name Cape Cod, Great Salt Lake, Great Slave Lake, Boston, Halifax, Los Angeles, Pittsburg, Winnipeg; sketch the course of and name the rivers Colorado and Yukon; and draw the boundaries of Mexico.

3. Compare the basin of the Saskatchewan-Nelson with that of the Mississippi-Missouri, as regards (a) extent, (b) climate, (c) commercial value.

4. In what parts of North America is there (a) a great range of air-temperature, (b) a Mediterranean type of climate, (c) very heavy summer rainfall? What effect has each of these conditions on the plant life?

5. On an outline map of North America, mark by various colours: the grass regions, tundra, coniferous forests, and evergreen forests. Show clearly the districts in which wheat, maize, and rice are cultivated; and the districts in which dairy farming is the chief industry.

6. From a 'Year Book' find the value of the annual coal outputs of the United States, British Isles, and Germany. Have these countries always stood in their present order as regards coal output? Why should the present leading country occupy this position?

British North America

1. Trace on an outline map of Canada the international boundary. Mark (where necessary) and name the great lakes, the course of the St Lawrence, Newfoundland, Cabot Strait, Strait of Juan da Fuca, Rocky Mts., Red river, and Lake Winnipeg; Montreal, Halifax, Fort William, Saskatoon, Prince Rupert, and Victoria.

2. Describe a journey by water from the Strait of Belle Isle to Port Arthur, by naming the waters over which you would sail, the direction in which you would go, the towns you would pass, and the uses to which the surrounding country is put.

3. Compare as regards range of air-temperatures and amount of rainfall Vancouver, Winnipeg, and Montreal. Briefly describe the effect of the climate on the industries of the country and on the navigation of the rivers.

4. In what parts of Canada are minerals being extensively worked ? What are the minerals, and to what uses are they put ?

5. What is the area of land which the Canadian Government offers free to intending immigrants ? Compare the nature and condition of this land in Saskatchewan and northern Ontario.

6. In what parts of Canada has there been the greatest increase of population, as shown by the recent census returns ? To what causes do you attribute the increases and decreases ?

7. Where are the following places and for what are they noted : Ottawa, St John, St John's, Toronto, Regina, Edmonton, Nanaimo ? What industries are there in the neighbourhood of each of these towns ?

United States of America

1. On an outline map of this country, shade in the areas of highland, naming each. Indicate by thick lines and name the chief mountain ranges. Mark and name the courses of the Mississippi and its tributaries ; Sacramento, Red river of the North ; Florida, New Orleans, San Francisco, St Louis, Chicago, Pittsburg, Erie.

2. Draw a sketch map of the Atlantic coast of North America from the Gulf of St Lawrence to Cape Hatteras. Name the chief bays, capes, and islands. Insert and name the Appalachian Mts., and the rivers Delaware, Hudson, Mohawk, and Potomac ; Baltimore, Boston, Brooklyn, Pennsylvania, Washington.

3. Name the vegetable products of the United States, and the districts in which each is cultivated. To what use is each crop put ?

4. In what part of this country is the chief manufacturing district ? Name the industries and the chief towns in this district.

5. Under what advantages or disadvantages are the following minerals worked in this country : Gold, silver, iron-ore, petroleum ? Account for the continuation of the iron and steel trade at Pittsburg, even though most of the local ore has been used up.

6. How many negroes are there in the States ? Where do they live, and what is their chief occupation ? How did they come to inhabit these districts ?

7. Distinguish between the occupations of the people living in New York, New Orleans, Philadelphia, Washington, Chicago, Los Angeles, Duluth.

Central America

1. On an outline map of Central America, showing the boundaries of the various countries, name each republic ; insert and name the courses of the Rio Grande, San Juan, and river Chagres ; name the islands Cuba, Jamaica, Trinidad, and the Bahamas ; and mark the position of and name Mexico City, Vera Cruz, Havana, Belize, Kingston.

2. Why is it possible to cultivate in Central America such varied crops as coco-nuts, coffee, maize, and wheat? For what purpose are bananas cultivated, and from what port are large numbers of bananas sent to England?

3. Account for the decrease, prior to the outbreak of war in Europe in 1914, and the subsequent increase in the sugar output of the West Indies.

CHAPTER IX. SOUTH AMERICA

1. Compare this continent with North America as regards (a) latitude, (b) area, (c) build.

2. Name the chief river basins in South America ; state which river is the most valuable for navigation ; and give the name of one important town in each basin.

3. Shade an outline map of South America to show the district where there is (i) rain all the year round, (ii) summer rain, (iii) winter rain only, (iv) no rain.

4. Make a list of the most important vegetable products of South America, stating where they are extensively grown, through what ports they are exported, and the uses to which they are put.

5. Describe the course of the Amazon and name its chief tributaries. State what vegetable products of commercial value are found in its basin.

6. Write short notes on maté, cinchona, llama, nitrate.

7. Which countries of this continent have no coast-line? Describe the industries and towns of one of these countries.

8. Describe the chief railway routes of South America, illustrating your answer by a sketch map.

9. Describe a coasting voyage from Guayaquil to Buenos Aires, naming the countries passed on the way, and describing the general character and aspects of the coasts. Name four ports and three islands passed on the way, indicating the position of each.

10. In what way has the opening of the Panama canal affected the ports of South America and the trade routes?

11. Write a description of the British colonies in South America.

INDEX OF PLACE NAMES

For EU product safety concerns, contact us at Calle de José Abascal, 56–1°,
28003 Madrid, Spain or eugpsr@cambridge.org.

www.ingramcontent.com/pod-product-compliance
Ingram Content Group UK Ltd.
Pitfield, Milton Keynes, MK11 3LW, UK
UKHW012335130625
459647UK00009B/297